Narcissists

Disarming and Becoming the Narcissist's Nightmare. How to Change Your Self, Stop Being a Victim of Toxic People and Avoid Emotional and Psychological Abuse

By Dr. Christina Covert

Legal Disclaimer

The information contained in this book and its contents is not designed to replace any form of medical or professional advice; and is not meant to replace the need for independent medical, financial, legal, or other professional advice or services that may be required. The content and information in this book have been provided for educational and entertainment purposes only.

The content and information contained in this book have been compiled from sources deemed reliable, and they are accurate to the best of the Author's knowledge, information, and belief. However, the Author cannot guarantee its accuracy and validity and therefore cannot be held liable for any errors and/or omissions. Further, changes are periodically made to this book as needed. Where appropriate and/or necessary, you must consult a professional (including but not limited to your doctor, attorney, financial advisor, or other such professional) before using any of the suggested remedies, techniques, and/or information in this book.

Upon using this book's contents and information, you agree to hold harmless the Author from any damages, costs, and expenses, including any legal fees, potentially resulting from the application of any of the information in this book. This disclaimer applies to any loss, damages, or injury caused by the use and application of this book's contents, whether directly or indirectly, whether for breach of contract, tort, negligence, personal injury, criminal intent, or under any other circumstance.

You agree to accept all risks of using the information presented in this book.

You agree that by continuing to read this book, where appropriate and/or necessary, you shall consult a professional (including but not limited to your doctor, attorney, financial advisor, or other such professional) before using any of the suggested remedies, techniques, or information in this book.

Table of Contents

Introduction

Narcissism. It's a word we hear a lot today in our politics, our day to day work life and recreational activities. But what is a narcissist and who is a narcissist? Is there a narcissist living secretly in every one of us? This is the subject of this book. To take a long look at what narcissism is, who is one, how did they get that way?

We will begin with definitions and end with stories. We have all experienced narcissists in our lives, and we have probably all exhibited some form of narcissism ourselves. In Chapter One we will define the Narcissistic Personality Disorder, its symptoms, causes, complication, and diagnosis. We will explore the possibilities of being a narcissist without having NPD (Narcissistic Personality Disorder)

From there we will look at how the disorder is treated today, the history of the disorder and psychological theories around it as well as famous narcissists throughout history.

In Chapter Five, we'll explore the parts of ourselves that are narcissistic and what we can do to improve ourselves. There is a good form of narcissism in term of healthy self-esteem and there is a pathological form of narcissism that is destructive to both the narcissist and the people in their lives.

Chapters six through nine will help us to see what it is like to live with a narcissist and how to handle it. The narcissist did not choose to be a narcissist and we need to keep this in mind as look at the people in our own lives who have strong narcissistic tendencies. How do you live with a narcissist like the subject of Chapter six? How a highly sensitive person, or empath, survives the presence of a narcissist in their life is the subject of Chapter Seven.

Chapter Eight deals with the most vulnerable among us – our children – and their interactions with the narcissists in their your lives. What is the impact of growing up with narcissistic parents? Will that make the child grow up to also be a narcissist?

Chapter Nine gets us out of the relationship with the narcissist no matter who they may be. We learn how to deal with them in our work or family environments. We learn how to protect ourselves from their vitriol, just as the highly sensitive person must protect themselves.

In Chapters Ten and Eleven we will explore the ramifications of a culture becoming deeply immersed in narcissism and a sports world that has been coached by narcissists for decades.

By then you will have a very clear understanding of what narcissism is and who the narcissist is. You will see how commonplace narcissism is today and how devasting its effects are on all of us. We know that our self-esteem is important, but it should be healthy self-esteem.

We all need a positive ego, but it should be a healthy ego. We all need love and respect, people who look up to us and people we can look up to. A small dose of healthy narcissism is good for all of us. A society drowning in pathological narcissism with its lies, grandiosity, cruelty, and arrogance is not good for any of us.

Here's hoping this short look at narcissism helps you to improve your situations and your life.

Chapter 1

What is Narcissistic Personality Disorder?

What is Narcissistic Personality Disorder? Can I be a Narcissist if I do not have this disorder?

The Narcissistic Personality Disorder affects about one in sixteen adults – at least to the degree that they exhibit traits of the disorder in enough number to be diagnosed with the disorder. It is interesting to note that sixty to sixty-five percent of all the people diagnosed with NPD are men. Psychiatrists, psychologists, and social workers have seen an increase in recent years in the prevalence of the disorder. At the same time, it has become easier to diagnose. So, it is not certain if the number of cases is really increasing or if the number of diagnoses simply is.

What is this disorder? What does it look like? What are its causes, complications and how is it diagnosed? Narcissistic Personality Disorder or NPD is a mental disorder that results in low self-esteem, but an exaggerated sense of your own importance.

It seems to be a contradiction. How can you have an exaggerated sense of your own importance and low self-esteem at the same time? Actually, it's pretty common. There are over three million cases a year in the United States alone and as we have seen over 1.7 of these cases are male. The person with NPD needs all the attention and admiration of everyone in their world. They believe they deserve it. At the same time, they cannot deal with the smallest of criticisms.

A person suffering from Narcissistic Personality Disorder has every aspect of their live impact by the illness. They are constantly disappointed and angry when their need for absolute approval and admiration isn't met. Their relationships, their work, their social and financial status, no matter how good, are constantly underperforming as far as the narcissist is concerned. There is never enough.

You might be saying but everyone wants admiration and success. Everyone is selfish now and then. Everyone wants to be seen as special in others eyes. What makes a narcissist different? The answer is the extreme to which the person suffering from

NPD takes these things. No one matters beyond themselves. They have no sympathy and no empathy for anyone else. They don't think anyone else has any value beyond themselves.

If you help them, if you build them up, if you tell them they are always right and no one else understands how to solve the issues they face except them; then they will treat you well until you fall out of favor. Sooner or later you will fall out of favor. We will deal with this in the chapter on relationships with narcissists.

The difference between a selfish, self-absorbed individual and someone with a mental illness called NPD – is the extreme beliefs and behaviors of the person with NPD. The person with NPD has a long history of needing excessive admiration and approval. They have a long history of feelings of self-worth completely out of proportion with the reality of their lives. They have a long history of lacking any capacity for sympathy and empathy.

They take advantage of every situation and every person they can. They are charming and influential. They are obsessed with power, appearances, and success. It is all they think about. They believe no member of the opposite sex would ever turn down a proposition from them. They can do whatever they want. They are that important. This behavior occurs in every aspect of their lives. All of their behavior and thinking deviated from the cultural norm.

This pattern of thinking and acting crosses every boundary in their lives. It is seen as a pattern of thinking, of effect, of impulse control and interpersonal functioning. It is pervasive and it is inflexible. They can't just turn it off. This can lead to social impairment, career self-sabotage, relationship distress, and feed the underlying sense of poor self-esteem that they begin with.

Recent studies have found though that some people with Narcissistic Personality Disorder, don't have low self-esteem. For some of them, their internal sense of self is actually as out of proportion with reality as their external persona is. Their confidence and self-esteem might actually match the symptoms and behavior associated with their disorder. For these individuals finding a cure or workable treatment for their, NPD is an overwhelming challenge.

While we all love being admired and liked, the person with NPD needs this so desperately it can destroy their lives. Everyone likes to brag about something once in a while, but the narcissist is manipulative, cocky and demanding. They are obsessed with vanity and prestige. You deserve special treatment. You deserve power and you deserve adulation. Not admiration – adulation.

At the same time, you will never be satisfied. You will never be fulfilled. You will never really be happy. Despite all that self-confidence, arrogance, and high self-esteem, life will never live up to your expectations. Your relationships will be unstable. Your career will be unsatisfying. Your expectations and delusions of grandeur will keep you dissatisfied and always reaching for more, more, more.

Symptoms and Behavior

So, what are the symptoms of Narcissistic Personality Disorder? There are many and not everyone suffering from NPD will exhibit them all. Here are some of them.

- The person with NPD is easily hurt but reacts with rage. He has no tolerance for criticism. He makes excuses and does not take any responsibility for his actions. He will deny he did things there is a record of him doing.
- He sees himself as charismatic and a natural leader that others will follow. He believes he is the most important person in the lives of everyone he knows and everyone he meets.
- Persons with NPD are rude and snobbish while accusing everyone else of the same behavior. They are condescending and belittle people.

- They are bullies and liars.
- They associate themselves with others who will bring them more self-esteem.
- Exaggerate even lie about their accomplishments and achievements.

To recap the symptoms and behavior, the person with Narcissistic Personality Disorder:

An exaggerated sense of importance, thinking you are special, always thinking of unlimited respect, unlimited admiration, unlimited financial and career success, unlimited sexual conquest, secretly jealous of others, sense of entitlement.

The Narcissistic Personality Disorder is named after a very good looking young male named Narcissus. The Greek myth has him looking into a reflection pool, seeing himself and falling in love. The narcissist is in love with himself.

In addition to the symptoms previously mentioned, those with full-blown NPD try to monopolize all the conversations, intimate that they are close with many high-status people, and be disdainful when others talk about themselves instead of him. He can get inappropriately angry or rageful if criticized. Usually, all of their actions and words are calculated and deliberate. As previously mentioned, they are the classic bully.

Those who are pathologically narcissistic are always intolerant of other points of view, controlling, manipulative, uncaring of other's needs, indifferent to the effect of their behavior on others, self-absorbed of course and blaming. They will protect themselves at any cost. They derogate, devalue, blame and insult everyone else to protect their own ego.

When someone with NPD feels humiliated or shamed, they will react with anger, isolation, defiance or revenge. They live in a constant state of denial, defensiveness, devaluation, and idealization. You can have a lot of personality traits that appear to be or actually are narcissistic, but to have NPD the person has to display these traits all the time, be maladaptive and inflexible. They must have caused functional impairment all around them on a significant level and caused distress as well.

Causes of NPD

What causes this disorder? The answer is not an easy one. This is because the exact cause of this disorder is not known. There are and have been a wide variety of theories from Freud to the present. The most prevalent belief is that the disorder is a combination of things from childhood experiences to the ability to handle stress.

A very recent study showed that parents who overindulge their children and tell them how great they are without ever criticizing them can begin the growth of narcissism. It has also been found that NPD can last your lifetime, or it might only last through your early years and be gone by the time you enter later age.

NPD may be accompanied by clinical depression and/or anxiety which the patient may be medicated for. NPD is not associated with mania or substance abuse per se. It usually displays itself for the first time during the teenage years and when your boys, in particular, go through puberty. At this time, they might display narcissistic traits that may or may not be transient.

Lifelong NPD is pervasive, rigid, apparent and consistent. The symptoms are so severe that they get in the way of the person being able to establish any meaningful and healthy relationships. They can also get in the way of normal functioning at school, at work, in social gatherings. In order to meet the medical and psychiatric definition of Narcissistic Personality Disorder, a person must be so different from the regular cultural and social norms that it is clear there is something else going on.

Some of the things that might be involved in the causation of NPD include:

- Neurobiology – The connection between thinking, behavior and the physical brain. Less volume of gray matter in the left side of the brain than those who do not exhibit traits of NPD. The left side of the Anterior Insula in the brain is responsible for compassion, emotion, empathy, and cognitive function. It controls that connection between thinking, behavior and physical traits.
- Genetics – inherited traits and characteristics.
- Environment/Parent-child relationship consistently of mostly excessive praise or excessive criticizing. Parenting styles may have a lot to do with it.

Most scientists and psychiatrists now agree that all three of these factors are at play and the many of the characteristics of the disorder come to light when the young boy is in normal development stages but there is conflict in these phases. Negative interpersonal experiences or environment that can cause these conflicts might include:

- Having an overly-sensitive nature at birth.
- Having parents that feed this nature by excessive praise or excessive criticism or both.
- Parents or peers who teach him manipulative behavior and he sees it rewarded.
- Being severely abused as a child physically, sexually or emotionally.
- Unpredictable and unreliable parent care.
- Peers, family, parents overindulge him.
- Looks or abilities receive excessive parental praise.
- No realistic feedback about who you really are, only excessive admiration.

Most professionals believe it is a combination of these factors, genetics, brain matter and environment that causes NPS. It is called a biopsychosocial model of causation, meaning that no one thing is the cause but rather a combination of the factors we have already discussed.

Complications of NPD

We are inclined to think of Narcissistic Personality Disorder as only a mental thing or even just an egotistical bully. However, there are other complications that come with the disorder as with other mental disorders. It has a comorbidity rate that is fairly high – meaning there are several other disorders and diseases that those with NPD are susceptible to that can cause death.

Many people with Narcissistic Personality Disorder might also have depressive disorders, substance abuse disorders, bipolar disorder, borderline, paranoid, histrionic and antisocial personality disorders. Other complications that can arise from NPD include:

- Drug or Alcohol abuse.
- Problems with relationships.
- Physical Health issues.
- Issues at school or work.
- Depression or anxiety or both
- Suicidal behavior or thoughts.

These comorbidities and complications make it much more likely that someone with an NPD will kill him or herself. There is also a slight chance if you have NPD that you will "pass it on" to your children. It is more environment and less genetics in the eyes of most professionals.

Diagnosis of NPD

So how are people with Narcissistic Personality Disorder diagnosed? Narcissists don't think there is anything wrong with them remember? Unless they are abusing alcohol or a chemical substance, or are substantially depressed, they are not likely to think they need any type of treatment. They would never consider that they had a mental illness.

However, treatment can make life a lot better for someone with NPD if they follow through with treatment. Before you can get treatment, you have to be diagnosed. So, what makes for a diagnosis of Narcissistic Personality Disorder? There are no tests – lab work – that can diagnose a mental disorder. There is a Narcissistic Personality Inventory that many psychiatrists, social workers, psychologists, and medical professionals use to measure a person's narcissistic traits. This test of 40 questions, measures a person's need for power and attention.

NPD can show up in a child only 8 years old or a man in his 30's. Our culture itself becomes more narcissistic every day. An Ohio State study indicates that a large number of people in our culture do not believe that there is any problem with narcissism. They believe there is no problem with looking out for yourself first.

So, it takes a mental health professional to diagnose a major personality disorder of any kind, especially one as elusive as NPD. The diagnosis is made by a review and clarification of symptom and health history to see how close you match the criteria for making such a diagnosis.

When it comes down to it, falling into narcissism is not a good way to cope with the traumas of childhood or a lack of self-esteem. Narcissism creates a split between one's conscious beliefs and one's unconscious motivation. NPD only carries on the destructive behavior, suffering and dysfunction the person has experienced most of their life.

Megalomania versus NPD

Many of us when meeting someone who has NPD and we don't know it might simply label this person as a megalomaniac. Now, what is that? Is it the same thing as a narcissist? Actually, the Diagnostic and Statistical Manual of Mental Disorders 5th edition (or DSM-5) has classified narcissism and megalomania as forms of Narcissistic Personality Disorder.

We know that narcissism is self-love taken to an exaggerated and grotesque extreme and we can define megalomania as self-esteem and sense of self-worth, power, and attractiveness taken to an extreme. This means that although all narcissists are not necessarily megalomaniacs, all megalomaniacs are narcissists.

A narcissist who also has megalomania is a monster indeed, with an extreme sense of superiority, extreme bullying, and who talks excessively in a rambling manner. The biggest difference might be that megalomania is considered to be a delusional state. The person might even truly believe themselves to be a famous, gifted person or even a "god" – a "messiah".

At times megalomania is also considered a symptom of other paranoid or deep personality disorders. All we really need to know for our purposes is that a megalomaniac is a narcissist and a narcissist is not always a megalomaniac.

Narcissists without Narcissistic Personality Disorder

Yes, you can be a narcissist and not have Narcissistic Personality Disorder. Yes, you can be hypercompetitive and self-absorbed and not have Narcissistic Personality Disorder. The difference? You might have all the traits of NPD but it never causes any problems in your daily life,

The major proponents of this belief are a psychological school of thought called Object Relations. This school of thought included people like James F. Masterson and Otto Kernberg. They wrote about Object Relations throughout their careers and defined the difference between being a narcissist and having Narcissistic Personality Disorder.

The theory says if you have NPD you will see other people as objects and not people. They are not capable of what is called "Whole object relations". If you can have whole object relations then you are capable of seeing people in relation to yourself in an integrated, realistic and stable way.

Those with NPD divide people into two categories. Those that are worthless, defective, garbage and those that are perfect, flawless, entitled and special. People are either all good or all bad. People with NPD lack "Object Constancy" because they cannot stay constant in a positive relationship with those they do care about if they are disappointed, angry, or hurt by them.

The rule of thumb then was that if you have Object Constancy and Whole Object Relations you don't have Narcissistic Personality Disorder. If you can care about people and be constant in it, you don't have NPD. According to this school of thought, you can have many traits of narcissism without having NPD.

However, people with other personality disorders also can have narcissistic traits or characteristics. This only makes understanding or even diagnosing someone with NPD even harder and more confusing. People with other personality disorders also lack whole object relations and object constancy. These folks might be narcissistic, but they do not have Narcissistic Personality Disorder.

This may be the most difficult thing about NPD and the ability to diagnose and treat it properly. The bottom line is the person with NPD always divides the world into those two groups of people – the ones they respect and the ones they devalue. If you don't do that, then you have narcissistic traits but not NPD.

There are many reasons for this. Just a few of those reasons include:

- Though their behavior appears to match the symptoms of NPD, there could be a very different cause entirely under the surface of their emotional responses – another personality disorder for instance.
- Their behavior could be motivated by anxiety or a mental illness like schizophrenia.

- They might struggle with the characteristics of NPD but it is not ruining their life or relationships.

This may be the most difficult thing about NPD and the ability to diagnose and treat it properly. A person may appear to have the behavior caused by NPD but that behavior is caused by something else. The bottom line is the person with NPD always divides the world into those two groups of people – the ones they respect and the ones they devalue. If you don't do that, then you have narcissistic traits but not NPD.

Chapter 2

Treatment for Narcissistic Personality Disorder

What do you do then if you are diagnosed with Narcissistic Personality Disorder and you want to cure it? What if you don't have NPD but want to get rid of overbearing narcissistic tendencies? What is the treatment or cure?

The truth is, as mentioned in Chapter One, the person suffering from NPD is not likely to know it and is not likely to see a doctor about it or be officially diagnosed. There is nothing wrong with them, it's everyone else. There are studies showing that those with full-blown NPD hardly ever get treatment for it. It is those narcissists without NPD that seek treatment to make their lives and the lives of those they love a lot better.

It is critical for those with NPD to get treatment but it will require a lot of effort on part of those who love them to get them into any type of treatment. The other thing that appears to happen to get a person with NPD into treatment, is that they come for reasons other than NPD. Remember the person with NPD does not think they have NPD, so they present for treatment for something else like clinical depression, eating disorders, bipolar disorder or substance abuse.

No matter the reason it is critical to get these folks into treatment. There is no cure for Narcissistic Personality Disorder. It can be treated, and the person can have a successful life, but the disorder will always be there. There are no drugs for NPD either. It's just not that easy. The treatment is long term psychotherapy.

The person with NPD might also be suffering from anxiety and/or depression and there are drugs to treat those issues. If they have a substance disorder that can be treated also. But the prognosis for NPD itself is indeterminate. There have not been enough empirical and systemic investigations of results from either long term psychotherapy or any attempt at drug therapy.

We simply don't know what the prognosis is. Clinical practice guidelines are still being developed and treatment at this time is based on psychodynamic NPD models in clinical settings and not in real life. It is still centered in the psychotherapy model and has been ever since the 1960s when Kemberg and Kohut, mentioned in Chapter One, claimed it was effective with NPD patients.

Today's psychotherapy is modeled in metacognitive, transference and schema-focused treatments. This is more often than not, long term treatment and must be conducted with a therapist who is well versed and experienced in working with NPD. This is especially critical because unless the narcissist respects and looks up to the therapist, the treatment has no chance of working. If the person with NPD puts the therapist in that group of people he distains, the treatment cannot work.

At the same time, the health care or mental health professional needs to make sure they are showing respect for the way their patient sees himself and his importance in the world. They can't downplay it or they will lose him. The trick is that while doing this, the clinician must also avoid building up the patient's pathological thought patterns.

So, it is important that the clinician follows a plan that supports the patient's sense of self in the beginning and then breaks down step by step their vulnerabilities and the implications of their actions that come from an illness not evilness within the person. Increase the patient's self-confidence while breaking down his sense of entitlement. The truth is that most clinicians end up addressing the behavior and the symptoms rather than the personality disorder.

Positive transference of feelings to the clinician and an alliance between the therapist and the patient is not the best way to reach someone with NPD, because the patient cannot see the therapist as they really are. Instead, they see them as either someone to be revered or someone to be devalued. Either way, they cannot see the clinician as like themselves so positive transference cannot really take place.

The next challenge is to keep the patient in therapy long enough to make an actual difference. When the narcissist is being treated for another personality disorder like depression or substance abuse, they usually do not stay in therapy long enough. But even the narcissist that does not abuse drugs or alcohol, will feel cognitive dissonance with the therapy and drop out. Even if the clinician does everything right, it is very likely that the person suffering from Narcissistic Personality Disorder will discontinue therapy long before the therapist thinks he should.

Those who do stay in therapy begin to work on issues of depression, relationships, and life goals. In order to continue to this level, the therapist must have a really good sense of NPD so not to encourage counter-transference and for really understanding what the patient is telling them. This then lets the therapist assist the patient with a better understanding of themselves, their emotions and their responses to those emotions. Now the patient can begin to build something different in their lives, something real and healthy.

The patient will be able to change behavior and how he does interpersonal interactions. However, actually changing personality traits could take years of therapy. This is because you are trying to get the patient to be able to tolerate criticism, to maintain healthy, respectful relationships with their family and coworkers. You are trying to get them to minimize their desire for unrealistic goals and get them to understand their feelings and control their reactions to their feelings.

The person who succeeds in NPD psychotherapy will be the one who is open-minded about it, really wants to change, understands their disorder and has educated himself about it, and can stay focused on those goals. The therapist who succeeds with NPD patients does so most often with a combination of personal, group and family therapies.

This cocktail of family, group and individual therapies are not easy or comfortable for a narcissist. It's bad enough they have to talk to the therapist about this, but you want them to do so with strangers and family members? It takes this intensive, long term therapy to help the person with Narcissistic Personality Disorder to understand the damage this condition has caused them and the people in their lives. This must be done subtly and not openly, or the narcissist will reject it and the therapist with it.

The therapeutic atmosphere for NPD work must be oriented to the solution and non-judgmental. These are evidence-based therapy programs and they might include:

- Psychodynamic Therapy – evaluate past experiences and their effect on their relationships and life.
- Cognitive Therapy- replace distorted thinking with realistic thinking.
- Family Therapy – Heal the family not just the NPD and help him understand how his behavior has really impacted his family.

Inpatient Therapy?

Is there any value to inpatient therapy for the narcissist? Yes, absolutely. In fact, all NPD patients should be inpatient for the beginnings of their therapy. The break from the "normal" grandiosity with which they live is essential for their success.

They can receive much more intensive therapy, plus assistance with complications and other disorders they may have. The success rates for dealing with Narcissistic Personality Disorder in-house are much higher than with just psychotherapy. Not to mention that all the external distractions have been taken away, while the environment they are in is non-judgmental and supportive.

Conclusion

Even though there is no cure and no pharmaceutical remedy, there still can be tremendous growth and success for this improving the lives of the person struggling with NPD. Take your time, choose the right therapist. Do inpatient first then do the hard work of psychotherapy for as long as it takes, with whoever needs to do it with you. Maybe there is not a cure or a pharmaceutical fix, but you can get better.

Chapter 3

The History of Narcissism and Famous Narcissists

So far, we have looked at what narcissism is; the actual mental disorder or Narcissistic Personality Disorder, symptom, complication, diagnosis, and treatment. Now let's look at the history of the behavior and the disorder. Who first coined the term narcissist and who put the disorder in the psychology reference books? What famous psychologist worked in this field and who were and are famous narcissists today.

For the purpose of this chapter, we will be looking at historical or famous narcissists whether they were diagnosed with Narcissistic Personality Disorder or not.

History of Narcissism

The behavior that we call narcissism has been around since the beginning of human history, but the term, the concept and the disorder we call Narcissistic Personality Disorder are relatively new. As covered in Chapter One, narcissism in ordinary nonscientific or psychological terms is the pursuing personal gratification from egoistic vanity, from admiring yourself to the extreme.

Once again, as mentioned in Chapter One, Narcissism is named after a young man in a Greek myth who fell in love with his own image in a reflecting pool. His name was Narcissus. He eventually died from grieving over a love that did not exist.

 In medieval times and during the Renaissance, this image had a lot of influence over the thinking. In Metamorphoses, Ovid retells the tale and alludes to the story. This supposedly influenced Shakespeare's Sonnets and the term self-love was used for what Narcissus was feeling. Francis Bacon picked it up and used it in Pompey- as Cicero was said to call them, "lovers of themselves without rivals". Next came Byron early in the nineteenth century saying that self-love stings anything it stumbles on. Finally, Baudelaire talked about self-love as being like Narcissuses of fat-headedness.

Egotism became the new word for self-love in the mid-century and lovers of self were now egotists – with Freud use of the ego and the id. Narcissism then, as a concept, was coined and defined within the field of psychiatry, psychology and psychoanalytic theory, by none other than Sigmund Freud.

Nacke had used the term as early as 1899, but he meant a sexual pervert. Then in 1911, Otto Rank picked up where Freud left off, identifying the word as vanity and self = admiration moving it back into the psychological realm, where it has basically stated within Narcissistic Personality Disorder.

Still, no one had more influence on the use of the term and the psychology of the concept than Sigmund Freud. The year was 1914 and the essay was On Narcissism, where Freud introduced the concept and used the word. By 1968 the American Psychiatric Association included the Narcissistic Personality Disorder in its Diagnostic and Statistical Manual of Mental Disorders associated it with megalomania.

So, for a long time, NPD and Megalomania were considered to be the same thing. They are not as we have also previously referenced. All megalomaniacs are narcissists. Not all narcissists are megalomaniacs.

At the same time, narcissism has been defined as a social or cultural issue, more in the line of sociological study than psychological. This is because you can be a narcissist and not have Narcissistic Personality Disorder. You will find it listed among the three dark triadic personality traits of psychopathy, narcissism, and Machiavellianism. It is also considered one of the factors in trait theory, self-report inventories like MCMI – the Million Clinical Multiaxial Inventory. From the outset, narcissism has been considered a problem for individuals and social groups. It was the end of the nineteenth century and the term became a regular part of the language. The term is used in analytic writing more than anywhere else and perhaps more than any other word.

Just like with anything else as time goes on the meaning of words change. This has happened somewhat with narcissism too. The world today has come to mean anything on a continuum from healthy self-love to pathological sense of self.

In the Beginning

As we said, Sigmund Freud coined the scientific term and the disorder. He discussed it in terms of a history of megalomania and his theory that megalomania was infantile. He believed that as the person developed, they grew from egocentric to social in their orientations.

Others who felt megalomania was normal for children included Edmund Bergler, Otto Fenichel and more. Then in the latter half of the 20th century, a new theory came into being, one we have already discussed – object relations theory. These new theorists saw a defense mechanism in megalomania that would allow for therapy while Freud saw megalomania as a problem for psychoanalysis.

Some psychologist and psychiatrist saw megalomania as a part of the normal growth and developmental pattern of a child, while others like Kemberg saw it as pathological. The popular culture also considers megalomania and narcissism to be the same thing.

Once the concept was set loose into the culture it blossomed. Megalomania was seen in popular terminology, novels and movies to mean a very self-centered uncaring individual. Just one example is the character played by Nichole Kidman in "To Die For". She wants what she wants and she will do anything to get it including murder her husband. Those who saw the film rated this character a 9 or 10 on a scale that had a prototypical Narcissistic Personality Disorder person as a 10.

Some others in the field did not see NPD as a separate personality disorder but as one part of the continuum of personality disorders. Alarcon and Sarabia, writing on this claimed that NPD was not sociologically inconsistent, and more research needed to be done to consider it a dominant trait.

Yet the concept of narcissism was so central to Freud's thinking and his concept of psychotherapy. He considered narcissism to be a necessary development stage in growing from childhood to adulthood. In his work, he separated narcissism into Primary and Secondary Narcissism.

Primary Narcissism

In primary narcissism is the "desire and energy that drives our instinct to survive". For Freud, this included narcissism as more normal than it had been thought, just a part of growing and developing. Freud claimed that narcissism complemented "the egoism of the instinct of self-preservation". What was meant by this was we are born without ego or a sense of ourselves as separate individuals. Then we develop the ego and primary narcissism until society intrudes with its norms and standards to insist that we develop an ideal ego – or move away from primary narcissism. The ego should aspire to a perfect self, one that can move to cathect objects. Freud defined the ego libido like that which is directed only toward oneself. Objed-libido is that which is directed toward other people or other objects that are outside of the self.

Secondary Narcissism

Secondary Narcissism occurs when the self-moves away from those objects and people outside of itself, especially their mother.   This leads the self toward the possibility of megalomania. Secondary narcissism which is not healthy is imposed upon primary narcissism which is healthy. Both of these types of narcissism develop in the normal course of human growth, but issues with transitions can lead to Narcissistic Personality Disorder when you become an adult.

Freud believed the self/ego had only a certain amount of energy and if it was turned toward objects or people outside itself then there would not be any left for narcissism. As a person develops, they move away from primary narcissism to giving their love away to others instead of keeping it for themselves.

 This is healthy development and the more love received in return, the less likely the person is to become pathologically narcissistic. To care for someone else is to transfer the ego-libido to an object-libido by giving away one's self-love. If this love is not returned, or it is disrupted then the individual's personality balance is upset and the potential for a psychological upset.

Beyond Freud

Following this, Karen Horney presented a very different view of narcissism than that put forward by mainstream psychoanalytic theorists such as Kohut and Freud. Her view of narcissism did not include primary Narcissism but rather posited that narcissism came about from the kind of early environment that poisoned the ability of the child to develop a healthy personality. Karen Horney believed that narcissism is not inherent in human nature.

Then along comes Heinz Kohut and his theory that a child is only fantasizing about having ideal parents and a grandiose self. He theorized that we all believed in perfection in ourselves and anything we participated in. This belief in the grandiose self becomes healthy self-esteem and the child's core values come from idealizing the parents.

Kohut believed that if the child is then traumatized, the child reverts back to the most primitive version of the narcissistic self. That version then remains primary for that person as they grow to adulthood. This becomes a Narcissistic Personality Disorder. The child does not relate to the external object but rather unites with their own idealized self-object.

He also believed that you would or could get beyond pathological narcissism either through analysis or the experiences of life. He felt if you could get beyond the pathology, you could develop ambition, ideals, and resilience for the good.

Next comes Otto Kernberg who though narcissism was simply the role the self-played in regulating one's self-esteem. He thought infantile narcissism was normal as long as the child was exposed to the affirmation of self and "acquisition of desirable and appealing objects". These objects would then become a part of the individuals mature and healthy self-esteem. Narcissism becomes pathological if infantile narcissism does not develop into healthy self-esteem for whatever reason.

Other important theorists since Freud include Melanie Klein, Herbert Rosenfeld, D.W. Winnicott and the French with Lacan, Bela Grumberger and Andre Green.

Narcissistic Personality Disorder Today

Today the DSM-IV contains Narcissistic Personality Disorder but there have been requests to remove it and submerge the condition into antagonism personality type domain. NPD it the "it" disorder of the twenty-first century. How will history remember our foray into this condition? There are now subtypes of narcissism that were not around before. Just to name a few, there are antisocial, prosocial, idealizing, mirroring, malignant, vulnerable, grandiose and exhibitionist.

NPD is a diagnosis that becomes more common every day. Is it just trendy or is it for some reason more prevalent? Do we truly have a "Culture of Narcissism" as Christopher Lasch proposed in his 1979 book by the same name? He believes that NPD has become the typical way of living in American culture today.

Now let's look at some people who throughout history have for one reason or another been labeled as narcissists or diagnosed with Narcissistic Personality Disorder in Chapter 4.

Chapter 4

Famous Narcissists

Who are the narcissists today? Do they suffer from Narcissistic Personality Disorder or a lesser form of the condition that does not control their lives or make them dysfunctional? Is the 46th President of the United States a narcissist as some as said? Who throughout history since Greek times of the myth of Narcissus is considered narcissistic? Let's take a look.

Everyone has what Freud called normal or primary narcissism, or the impulse to take care of ourselves and have healthy self-esteem. This is very different from pathological narcissism, or secondary narcissism where one withdraws from all objects and persons, focusing only on self-love and megalomania. This is really just primary narcissism magnified to the extreme as Narcissistic Personality Disorder.

If Narcissistic Personality Disorder or lesser forms of pathological narcissism are abnormal mental disorders in which the individual exhibits a grossly exaggerated self-image, delusions of grandeur, a sense of oneself as almost a god.

Someone who believes themselves to have immense wealth, power, fame or importance. This person will lie about their resources, who they know, their experience, their wealth – anything to appear great to everyone else.

Here are some historical figures, in no particular chronological order, and no particular order of importance, who fit into these categories. Some of these people are harmless to society, other people and themselves, but they may be obnoxious to live with. Others listed here are monsters to society, other people or themselves.

There is no question however that throughout the course of history and certainly in the world today, there are and have always been narcissists.

Before the 20th Century

1. Napoleon Bonaparte: So many times, Napoleon has been labeled as suffering from "Little Man Syndrome" – actually created in his name. You have also, I'm sure, heard of the "Napoleon Complex" – referring to his low self-esteem and sense of inferiority that caused him to be a power-hungry, arrogant tyrant, with delusions of grandeur and his sense that he was special.

2. Alexander the Great: The only reason Alexander went to war was to show how great he was and to meet his own ambitions. It was all about glory and conquest and not for anyone else's glory but his own. He was emotionless in the face of the agony and death of his army. He named more than 70 cities in his own names. He had a deep-seated need to be great.

3. King Henry VIII: He was as charismatic and charming as any narcissist. He was also considered to be one of the egotistical and cruel leaders in human history. He beheaded some wives and discarded many others in order to have a male heir. He had no empathy and was extremely vain about the way he looked.

4. King Herod: Egotistical enough to kill all the baby boys in the kingdom in order to assure that no other potential king could be born. He killed his father-in-law, two sons, and several wives. He had uncontrolled ambition and jealousy.

5. Casanova: Was Casanova a serial rapist or an extreme charmer of women? We may never know but he certainly was a narcissist. All his energy was focused on his own pleasure and his own self -love. He felt nothing for the women he seduced, only for his ambition and pride.

6. Marquis de Sade: The Marquis shared many traits with Casanova only the Marquis was a sadist. Yes, he was a revolutionary, a nobleman, a writer, and a philosopher. Yet he is known for his erotica and his sadistic relations with women. He, like Casanova, had an ego that would not let him believe there was a woman anywhere who did not want him and his tastes in sex.

7. Elizabeth Báthory Countess of Transylvania: Accused of being a serial killer of hundreds of girls. She was said to bathe in the blood of virgins to maintain her youth and beauty. Everything was all about her. She had no empathy for anyone else.

8. Virginia Oldoini the Countess of Castiglione: She was obsessed with her own beautiful and had hundreds of portraits of herself painted over her lifetime. Like

Narcissus himself, she was known for spending much time observing herself in a mirror and having her portraits contain the image of her observing her face in the mirror.

9. Marie de Medici Queen Consort: As Queen of France and her reputation is based on all her political intrigue to keep her family and her name alive and on the throne of France. Power was her motivation and she believed that she and her Medici dynasty were the only ones who deserved to rule.

10. Marie Antoinette: Known most for words she might or might not have said, Marie Antoinette's famous quote about her hungry subjects, "let them eat cake", is a good indication that no one mattered outside her circle

11. Cleopatra Thea: Known as one of the strongest women leaders in early history Cleopatra showed many traits of the typical narcissist. She thought she was invulnerable. She flaunted her beauty, she broke the rules at will, she thought she would never

have to answer for it. Vanity and power were the motivators of her life.

12. Julius Caesar: Like all the Roman Emperors, Julius Caesar believed he was the embodiment of a god. He should be adored and worshipped, his image on the money of the empire. He did a lot of positive things for the empire, but his motivation was always his power, his reputation, and his legacy.

From the 20th Century to Today

1. Jim Jones: his narcissistic preacher killed hundreds at Jonestown, South Africa simply to prove they would do whatever he told them to because he was their god. He torture his followers when anyone did anything he did not approve of. He was all about power and charisma. He truly believed he was the messiah.

2. Adolf Hitler: We are all familiar with the monster that was Hitler. He was perhaps the worst dictator of the 20th century killing more people than history has probably recorded. Millions of innocent people died to satisfy Hilter's ego and his belief that he was the head of a master

race. With no empathy for anyone, including those closest to him, he demanded total obedience. Anyone who he felt was not like him, was subject to death.

3. Joseph Stalin: He might give Hitler a run for his money as a dictator and murderer. His pride and ego caused the death of many and trusted no one. No one was worthy of his trust. He was the first Communist leader in Russia who eliminated all political opposition. He could not tolerate anyone who criticized him. Stalin was obsessed with his own vanity, power, and prestige.

4. Idi Amin: In these 20th-century leaders we are seeing the worst of what a Narcissistic Personality Disorder can do. As president of Uganda, Amin killed hundreds if not thousands. He awarded himself the highest British award for bravery, the Victoria Cross.

5. Czar Nicholas: Another leader of Russia who only cared for himself and his family. His ego and pride led to the death of many members of ethnic groups and Jews, for the same reason as Hitler. They were not like him. He believed his kind was better than anyone else.

6. Rasputin: As a priest and a confidant of the Tsar of Russia's wife. He is not known as a full-blown narcissist but rather a megalomaniac. He was consumed with power rather than vanity and charisma. His desire was not to be loved but rather to be feared.

7. Chairman Mao of Communist China: Another of the murderous dictators of the 20th century. Mao led the purges in Communist China during the Cultural Revolution. Thousands died to satisfy Mao's need for everyone to be the same – be the way he ordered them to be. His ego and pride demanded that uniformity in everything would be his legacy; that he would do communism better than Russia or anyone in Southeast Asia.

8. Charles Manson: One of the most notorious narcissistic mass murders in recent US history, even though the numbers of people his family killed were not nearly as many as other serial killers.

9. Saddam Hussein: So many narcissistic leaders in the 20th and 21st century are dictators and terrorists, responsible for the deaths of thousands of people.

10. Joseph Mengele: This narcissist was known as the "angel of death" and was responsible for the gas chambers and sadistic experiments on men, women, and children. He had no remorse, enjoyed other's pain because it exemplified his power. Mengele was all about power.

11. Kayne West: Known to say he is the Messiah, Saviour, and Yeezus. He has no empathy and thinks only of what matters to him. He stood at one of his concerts and demanded that the audience stand and applaud him. He called out audience members who did not stand. He belittled one audience member who was in a wheelchair, but Kayne did not apologize.

12. Ted Bundy: One of the most egotistical of all the serial killers we have discussed. He was a master of manipulation, vain, charismatic, and filled with delusions of grandeur. He really believed he was the master of the perfect crime and no one would ever catch him. He had many traits of a Narcissistic Personality Disorder.

Nothing was more important than being the center of attention.

Sports Coaches

Finally, there is a whole group of other narcissists that because they "win", our society tolerates them in the same way that we tolerate many of our professional politicians. Both groups – coaches and politicians – are supposed to be leaders, someone that young people look up to. Both groups – politicians and coaches – have more than their share of narcissists and those who have a Narcissistic Personality Disorder.

Most of the names on this list need no introduction. All of them have bullied their teams and individual athletes. All of them demand respect beyond their position and accomplishments. They expect to be adored, admired, obeyed in everything. Most of all they expect to win and if their teams do not win, it is not their fault. It is the fault of the team or individuals on the team, or the institution they work for.

Speaking of the institution – they are above the law at that institution – no one can touch them no matter what they do. This is their egotistical belief. The institution needs them far more than they need it.

The list is not complete in any way. It is just a simple sample.

Conclusion

History is full of stories about narcissists and those with a full-blown case of Narcissistic Personality Disorder. We have only touched the surface in this chapter. How many of the world leaders today fall into this category? How many killers are narcissists? How many more?

Chapter 5

Recognizing the Narcissist in Ourselves

Are you a narcissist? Am I? Is the premise of Christopher Lasch's 2018 book, "The Culture of Narcissism: American Life in An Age of Diminishing Expectations" on target? Is or has America become a nation of narcissists?

Tough questions and even tougher if you are a narcissist as you are not going to admit to anything that will get you criticized. So, until you know more and know who to blame, you could not possibly admit to being a narcissist. So how do we go about recognizing the narcissist in ourselves?

Narcissism itself can run on a scale of having one narcissistic trait to having Narcissistic Personality Disorder. If you have one trait, that isn't likely to make you a narcissist, but what if you have six? Is being a narcissist entirely wrong? We have seen Freud talk about the positive or primary narcissism. We know that plenty other psychologists, psychiatrists, and scientists agree with Freud on this and very few have opposed him.

In our culture today it is very difficult if not impossible to not have at least one or two of the traits of narcissism. Does that make you a narcissist or is there a continuum of traits? If there is a continuum at what point does someone become a narcissist? Maybe it is quality, not quantity? Maybe you are a narcissist if you are very extreme in the few traits you have rather than needing 8 traits to be labeled as such.

When it comes to this subject there seem to be more questions than answers. Maybe that is why there seems to be so much interest in the subject. Most children growing up today receive an abundance of criticism along with praise, but more often it is the criticism that sticks with us and makes us ask "Am I good enough?". It is this negative self-esteem and self-criticism that can turn a blooming child into a festering narcissist.

On the other side of that coin in our "everybody wins" society, many parents never criticize their children. These children are golden and can do no wrong. These children will grow up to believe they are still golden and can do no wrong. These children grow up with the ego of a narcissist and the sense of entitlement we have been speaking of.

In her article, "Are We All Narcissists?", Shannon Thomas, claims that everyone, while not being a narcissist, displays narcissistic traits and behaviors throughout our lives. Let's remind ourselves of the traits of narcissism.

Traits of Narcissists

- Arrogance
- Grandiosity
- Manipulation
- Sense of Entitlement
- Selfishness
- Envy
- Attention Seeking
- Unable to accept constructive criticism
- Lack of Empathy
- Self-absorption
- Delusions of Greatness
- Entitlement
- Craving praise and admiration

Take a look at this list again. Yes, it is a generalized and simplified lay term for the symptoms of narcissism, but how many times today have you already indulged yourself with one or more of these traits? Look more closely.

Were you self-absorbed when someone else was trying to talk to you or needed you? Were you cocky and certain you would win the argument because you are "always right"? What does it mean to be arrogant and self-serving? Aren't most of us that at least a few times a week if not a few times a day?

The difficulty with narcissism isn't just that its traits exist in almost all of us, but rather how often each one of us displays one or more of these traits. We are all on the continuum of narcissistic traits, but we are certainly not narcissists. Let's look again, more closely at what each trait means and the type of behavior that goes with it. As we do think about your behavior today or yesterday? Was it narcissistic or just normal human behavior? How do you know?

As you look again at this list think deeply about how it might apply to you. Be fair. Don't under or overestimate your motivations. Perhaps you should ask someone else who is close to you to tell you how much you display that particular trait.

Look carefully at your history and try to reach your subconscious. Does being below average mean the same thing as failing? Did your family set the standards so high when you were a child that you can never succeed? IF you find this to be true you might want to moderate what looks like narcissistic behavior so you can be good enough and let go of this behavior.

- Arrogance: Appearing to be better than others; to know more than others; to always have the answers. We all do this at times. At times we are the ones with the answers, so it is hard to distinguish. Conceited. Vain.

- Grandiosity: Overconfident? Cocky? Do you exaggerate your accomplishments or your history? Showing off. Bragging. How many times a week? A day? Yes, you can have and need to have a healthy pride. IF you need to impress others though you may have a problem.

- Manipulation: How do you really see others? Do you see others as a means to your ends? What can you get from the relationship? What can you get them to do for you? Do you ever think about what they might get from a relationship with you? These thoughts might not be conscious ones so look deep for your own motivations.

- Sense of Entitlement: What do you really believe you are entitled to? If you feel like failure might you develop a sense of entitlement to compensate for that. As infants, we are entitled. We are entitled to care, to food, to our survival needs being met. When the emotional needs we are entitled to are not met it results in an emotional scar that psychologists call a "narcissistic injury". Creating an adult sense of entitlement give us the reassurance and love we didn't get as a child.

- Selfishness: It's ok to be self-nurturing but do you take it to far? Do you put yourself above everyone else? You could do this without realizing it and without knowing that you were being unfair.

- Envy: How about wanting what others have and being very envious of them while fantasizing that they are envious of you? It's ok to wish for things we don't have. It's not ok to want what one specific person has and be obsessed with it.

- Attention Seeking/Craving praise and admiration: Think about this? Do you try to get others to compliment you?

Do you spend your time with people who give you admiration and attention? Do you avoid those who do not seem to look up to you?

- Status Seeking: Do you intentionally try to get close to people of status, celebrity or power? If so, do you tell everyone you know that you know the senator, the rock star? Is it important to you that others know you are in touch with these people of status?

- Unable to accept constructive criticism: Are you overly sensitive to constructive or other types of criticism? Do you lash out at the critic? If your ego is fragile you may overreact to criticism. Do you blame those who criticize you and try to belittle them? Do you have problems with anger? Are others afraid of you?

- Lack of Empathy: Do you care what other people feel or are going through? Are you only concerned with what matters to you? Are you able to identify with others and do you even want to or are all your relationships built on what others can do for you?

- Delusions of Greatness: Do you think you will have great wealth or beauty? Do you fantasize that you are adored by all and have unlimited power? If this is your fantasy life you are unconsciously acting out of something that happened when you were young.

All of us have narcissistic tendencies and maybe more in the United States these days than ever before. However, you can get rid of these tendencies if you are really honest with yourself and look deeply at these things and what caused them.

A Narcissistic Culture

Whose fault is it? Who can we blame for the way things are? Who could stand up against the evil in the world? Who is to blame? The narcissists of course. All they care about is themselves and the rest of us can be tossed away. The state of the environment, the wars around the world it's all the work of the evil narcissists or at least that is what you hear these days.

Everyone is a narcissist and the narcissists are to blame for everything that is wrong in our world. Yes, yes of course they are. Joan Crawford, Henry VII, Hitler, Stalin, Osama bin Laden are just a few of those who are true narcissists and influenced our world. It is not very likely that you are one of them.

You do live in a culture that in itself is becoming more narcissistic by the day. Some would say it is because our leader is a narcissist but the changes to our culture were well underway before Donald Trump became president. Those changes may even have contributed to his becoming president.

Everywhere you look in America today you see signs of narcissism. Everyone wants everything right now. You better not disrespect me or I will beat you up for it. You are so stupid! I can do that so much better than you are doing it. Everyone is going around calling everyone else a narcissist and this is dangerous.

You and I are probably not narcissists. It's even likely that Donald Trump has narcissistic tendencies but is not a narcissist but has many narcissistic tendencies. But does he have Narcissistic Personality Disorder? No one knows. NPD is a serious, actual mental disorder that cannot be diagnosed by laymen. It is as we have seen difficult to diagnose. It is rare it is not common. Millennials are not more narcissistic than Baby Boomers or GenxERS. In reality, the number of persons with full-blown Narcissistic Personality Disorder has not increased in 20 years.

There are a lot of problems in our world but rampart Narcissistic Personality Disorder is not one of them.

Chapter 6

Living with a Narcissist

We know a lot about narcissism now. We know what it is and the history associated with it. We know a lot of famous people who have had Narcissistic Personality Disorder or have been on the narcissistic continuum. We've talked about the symptoms, the causes and how it is diagnosed.

We know it can't be cured and is not usually treated pharmacologically, though comorbid or complicating conditions and personality disorders can be. We also learned that there is a little bit of narcissism in everyone.

Knowing all this, what do you do if you find yourself in a relationship with a narcissist – even if that person is your spouse or life partner? By now you should know how to tell. However, you might not have known it when you committed yourself to this relationship and by now your partner might have convinced you that it is you who are crazy, not them.

Living with a narcissist is not easy. In fact, it is terribly hard. You know a narcissist is all about himself. You know a narcissist is almost always male – about 90%. He is probably vain, selfish, arrogant and manipulative. He thinks he is perfect and wants the world to think you think he is perfect. He can be mean, belittling and destructive. When you got involved with him, he did not show you his true self. He didn't do that until he was sure he had you hooked – married or not.

Why Are You Living with a Narcissist?

He was charming, handsome, kind when you met him. You fell head over heels and no wonder. Narcissists can be the most charismatic people on earth. He showered you with gifts; told you what a great life he could give you with his position, money, and status. You thought you were with the best man on earth.

Then something happens and he flips. Suddenly you see the real guy – the angry, selfish, self-centered egomaniac that he really is. Who is this guy you wonder and what will it take to change him back? The bad news is once he has let his guard down and let you see the megalomaniac that he really is, there is no going back.

It doesn't really matter what caused the change – marriage, job change, children, or some other life change – the change will now be permanent. You are now partnered with a completely different person than the one you knew before. He is demanding, critical and demeaning. He is drinking more and more. The more he drinks the meaner he gets. Yet in public, he is still the same charming, handsome, charismatic guy you fell in love with and you can see other women and men responding to him as you once did. No matter all of this, you are still in love with him. No matter how he abuses you, you are still in love with him.

Living with a narcissist is extremely hard. It can be even harder to change it. Getting out of a relationship with a narcissist that you still love or used to love is even harder. We will deal with what it takes to actually leave a relationship with a narcissist in another chapter. In this chapter, we are dealing with surviving while living with someone with a Narcissistic Personality Disorder.

Surviving Living with a Narcissist

While you are still involved in this relationship and living with this narcissist, how do you survive? While you are processing what is happening you have to deal with it at the same time until you are ready to leave the relationship. You are not just being abused; you are being used. Your role now is to make him happy or feel powerful and elite. You have to take the blame for everything he does that comes out wrong and anything you do that doesn't fit his image of himself and his perfect relationship or family.

They are always, always right and you are always, always wrong. On and on it goes until you really do think that you are crazy and he must be right. This is the classic battered woman syndrome, even if he never lays a hand on you. He is the classic bully, the classic narcissist. You begin to doubt yourself and everything you do. You try harder to make him happy. You try with all your might to bear the burden of his disease, even though you still don't even know that he has a disease.

The truth is he probably doesn't know it either. He has always been this way. IT's just how he thinks. It's just how he *is*. Even he might not know any better. That doesn't change the fact that his behavior is unacceptable. He is incapable of empathy. He can't see life through another person's eyes. He believes his own exaggerations and he hates you if you try to dissuade him of them.

He only wants to be with people he thinks are worthy of him and on the same status level as he perceives himself to be. He has to put people down when he is with these "higher status" people. Living with this is hard, but it can be done. You just have to know that his mind does not work the same way yours does. Everyone has narcissistic tendencies as we saw in the previous chapter. Yet living with a full-blown narcissistic personality is an entirely different story.

Making it Work

How can you make it work and survive in this situation?

- Try to stay positive – this is incredibly difficult in the situation you are in, but it is the first step in regaining some control over your life. Don't argue with him. Try to be positive without annoying him even more. Try to remember that many narcissists have poor self-esteem and they do the things they do to make themselves feel better, not to make you feel bad.

  If you remember from earlier chapters on Narcissistic Personality Disorder and Freud's work as well as others, he doesn't really think of you at all. He can't see you as an object or person outside of himself. So try not to internalize his abuse.

- Make space for yourself – Find a way to make your own place/space among the chaos and confusion. Knowing you can't leave the situation, find a place of peace and calm within it. Make yourself a sanctuary. The more you can stay beneath the radar, the better it will be.

- In any conversation, let the narcissist have the last word as this is likely to avoid any arguments or give the person with NPD a chance to abuse you verbally. Give him what he wants as much as you can in public.

- Establish clear boundaries – you can avoid him as he is your life partner, so you have to establish at least a few boundaries. First of all, you need to keep yourself safe. Build whatever walls you have to emotionally with a positive attitude. Then establish small boundaries. If he is always demanding money from your paycheck and he has plenty say no. If he is always demanding that you go everywhere with him and you need some space say no. Avoid as many arguments as you can in order to avoid the emotional abuse, but start to say no. Not everything all at once, but one "no" at a time.

- Be honest and true to yourself – speak your truth – when you are hurt by his words tell him. If you want to cry, cry. The point is to make it clear without anger that what he is doing is not ok. You do not have to take it. This goes along with the setting of boundaries. Don't hide your emotions.

- See a therapist – whether you can get your narcissistic partner to go with you or not, see a therapist on your own. Sure, it would be best if you both went to a therapist together but if not, you have to go. See a therapist for your own sake. You need someone to talk to. You cannot deal with this – you cannot deal with any type of mental illness in a family member by yourself – but this is particularly true of Narcissistic Personality Disorder. A therapist can teach you things you can do to combat the negativity in the relationship and to keep yourself on an even keel with your own self-esteem intact and healthy.

- Learn about narcissists and Narcissistic Personality Disorder – it will help you if you understand more about this disorder. Learn what the traits and the symptoms are so you know what to expect from your partner. The more you learn, the easier it will be to believe that none of this is your fault. You can learn not to internalize anything he says to you or accuses you of.

You still love this person and you are trying to understand him on a much deeper level than ever before. Understanding NPD is the biggest step you can take toward understanding him.

Knowing that his narcissism might be genetic, biological or caused by trauma in his childhood is a great help in not only understanding him but in coping with his behavior. If either of his parents also suffered from Narcissistic Personality Disorder, it could have been genetically passed on to him. It is also possible that whatever behavior his parents exhibited toward him, whether they were narcissists or not, could have damaged him enough to cause his own NPD.

- Learn coping skills – learn from your therapist and from your new knowledge of Narcissistic Personality Disorder. Again, regardless of the type of personality disorder, someone has, if you live with them, you need coping skills and support. One coping skill may be to remember as in the previous point, that his behavior untreated, maybe beyond his control.

- Create a sense of humor about your life and relationship. This is a coping skill. You can use humor to diffuse situations that occur where your partner is acting with disdain, belittling you or others. Just smiling makes the person wearing the smile, to feel better than they did before. Prepare in advance. If he says you don't cook well, laugh and agree with him. Turn the tables, Suggest that you take some cooking classes. Do it lightheartedly with a smile. Now instead of an argument, you've let him think he was right and made a joke of it. Make a list of things you can say when things get tense or begin to spiral out of control. Deflate the whole situation before it gets started.

- Join a support group – you need this as much as you need the therapist. Maybe even more. Here you will learn you are not crazy and none of this is your fault. Living with someone with a mental illness is incredibly difficult and you need support. When you consider all that has been said about the narcissist and their behavior in relationships, you can see that this would be even more important dealing with someone with Narcissistic Personality Disorder.

Given how manipulative your narcissistic partner can be, and that you had lived in this relationship for years without even knowing he was ill; some of his cruel criticisms had to be ingrained in you. Just knowing about his Narcissistic Personality Disorder will not erase these cruel beliefs from your mind.

A support group can keep you centered and grounded in who you really are and not who your partner tells you, you are. You can go to an in-person support group or you can join an online one. Either will give you the support and grounding that you need.

- Know when to walk away – in a later chapter we will talk about how to walk away.

Here are a few additional tips:

1. Don't let a narcissist live off of promises. This could fall into the boundaries area but make sure you get action and not just a promise. A narcissist is great at boasting and making promises and not so good at acting on them. It's

important to hold him accountable. This is one of the boundaries he can't cross.

As charming and manipulative as a narcissist can be, they will only act on what benefits them. If your relationship with him benefits him, then he is likely to promise anything in the heat of a moment. He has no intention of keeping those promises. Again, if he benefits from his relationship with you, then he needs to act on what he promises. Hold him accountable. Tell him you are not accepting any promises only action. Tell him this is a line in the sand and mean it. You also have to follow through.

2. On the issue of boundaries mentioned previously, this is a really important mechanism for living with a narcissist or someone with full-blown Narcissistic Personality Disorder. In order for both of you to be clear about what your boundaries are, write them down.

Find that sacred place we talked about earlier where you can be alone and away from your partner. Take the time to sort out what really matters to you. What are the boundaries? What are the lines you will not cross or allow to be crossed? Boundaries are things you won't accept him doing, things you won't do, your private time, whatever else matters to you.

If you do this, you have to be prepared to follow through yourself. You have to be prepared for his reactions when you say no; when you turn away and don't give them the attention and praise, they need. You have to know what you are willing and able to actually follow through on – what will you act on – if he crosses the boundaries.

3. On the point of understanding the narcissist you are living with – the narcissist believes in perfect love because of course he is entitled to perfect love and who could resist giving it to him. This need for perfect love comes from all the unresolved pain and trauma from his childhood. Those of us without a mental illness or disorder, understand that unconditional, perfect love is never really attained on a day to day

basis without a lot of giving and take. The narcissist, however, expects his true love to approve of everything about him unquestionably. He expects a perfect union where it all revolves around him and his partner gets swallowed up by him.

If and when this doesn't happen, he is angry and hurt. He feels vulnerable and reacts angrily to that feeling. He buries his feelings and becomes even less capable of empathy than ever. Love is not possible without empathy and we know that the narcissist does not have any. When their idealized love doesn't come about, they become abusive. The only emotions they allow themselves to feel is anger and rage. Since they are incapable of a healthy way of dealing with confrontation and conflict; since they are incapable of real give and take love; they become possessive, shut down even more emotionally and protect themselves.

Protecting Yourself

Knowing all you now know, if you choose to live with a narcissist, you need to protect yourself. Don't define your self-worth by what anyone else thinks, says or does. Easier said than done we know, but it is the only way to survive to live with a narcissist without causing yourself severe emotional damage.

Remember that self-esteem and self-worth are not imposed from outside but grow from the inside. Of course, external support and reinforcement help self-esteem to grow. You won't get this kind of support from the narcissist. In fact, if you confide in the narcissist, you are likely to find him using that information to manipulate you.

You can protect yourself by accepting that the narcissist is who he is and is not going to change. Understand his mental issues and accept his limitations. If you do love him and intend to stay in the relationship, you have to accept that he has Narcissistic Personality Disorder and these traits are deeply internalized in him. Accept his limitations. Be compassionate. Understand that he doesn't control this and underneath it all, he is very vulnerable.

You can protect yourself by listening without responding. Now you are giving the narcissist what he craves – attention. Just don't go overboard. Listen. Acknowledge. Keep yourself safe.

Chapter 7

How Does a Sensitive Person Deal with a Narcissist?

We know how difficult it is for the ordinary person to live with a narcissist. It is indeed hard, terribly hard. We know the narcissist is all about himself. The problem is the sensitive person or the empath is all about everyone but themselves. The narcissist has no empathy – no intuition – no openness to the other.

We know that the narcissist is vain, arrogant, selfish, and manipulative. He is mean, destructive and belittling. Whether you work with him, socialize with him, go to the same church or even maybe are in a personal relationship as a friend or lover, you are in danger around him.

People who are highly sensitive – empathic – are in real danger from all narcissists. You might even be a target for narcissists. No matter. Your duty to yourself is to stay as far away from any narcissist or person displaying Narcissistic Personality Disorder.

As an empath, you feel intensely and within every fiber of your body, whatever emotions are going on in the people around you.

The narcissist is a toxic personality and it is very difficult, very dangerous and very destructive for a sensitive, intuitive person. For you to be in any type of relationship with a toxic personality like a narcissist, is a very scary proposition. The narcissist is abusive and wants very much to manipulate you. He wants to blame you for everything wrong in his life or job or friendships.

He will always be right. If you enter into dialogue with him, you will always be wrong. You will also be in agony from the negativity he is putting out. He has the ability to make you crazy – not think you are crazy – actually drive you crazy. He may not even know that he has a mental illness. He may only know that he feels the way he feels. For him, his behavior is just his behavior, for you, it is much, much, more.

Who is the Sensitive Person? Who is the Narcissist?

Just who are we talking about here who will struggle with the narcissist? We can call this a highly sensitive person or we can call them an empath. No matter what we call it, it is a person who picks up the feelings of everyone around them. An empath is sensitive – a person who walks into a room and can feel what the people in the room are feeling. They know who is happy, who is scared, who is sad, and who is the narcissist. It isn't just that they feel who is feeling what…they don't just feel it they take it into their own bodies. The energy good or bad, the emotions intense and consuming, are absorbed by the sensitive/empath. Most of us are sympathetic and the other person's emotions are external to us. For the empath, the other person's emotions are taken into yourself and become a part of you. If you are not aware and careful, you can own these other emotions that are not yours at all.

This is the life of the empath and into this spacewalk a person whose emotions are toxic. Into this spacewalk a person who cares for no one but himself has no empathy – actually has no sympathy either. For the highly sensitive person to take on the energy field of a narcissist is frightening. The energy fields of others are felt by the empath. The energy of the empath vibrates at a frequency given off by the others in the room. Imagine the energy field of the highly sensitive person vibrating at the same frequency as the narcissist.

The empath is drained by this energy field of the other which is toxic. As you take on the emotions of others, you drain your own. When the energy is toxic, as it is with the narcissist, how drained will the highly sensitive person be? The only way that the sensitive person can truly deal with the narcissist is to shield them out. At the same time, there are other things the sensitive person can do.

The empath will be able to identify the narcissist in the room, or the person with full-blown Narcissistic Personality Disorder, by the way, they feel after interacting with them. Empaths instinctively give away their own energy and their own needs in favor of responding to everyone else's'. How did your interaction with that person make you feel? Did you feel at tug at your own self-esteem? Did you feel a little less self-confidence, a little less "worthy"?

Did you feel manipulated? Did you think this person was really interested in you or were they talking to you to see how you could be of use to them? What happened to your energy? Did it go down? Were you energized or drained by his presence in your energy field? The empath will know they are in the presence of a toxic narcissist. Now, what can you do about it?

Effects of the Narcissist on the Sensitive Person

The highly sensitive person is susceptible to any toxic personality, but as we know, the narcissist is the worst. What happens to an HSP who is overexposed to the toxic energy of the narcissist? What kind of symptoms does the highly sensitive person experienced in the presence of persistent narcissistic toxicity?

Starting with the intense feelings of negativity the HSP picks up from the NPD – there is a tendency to shut down. The empath will withdraw into themselves and hide. When this happens you no longer see the real person and interactions with the HSP become confusing. Even in this withdrawn stage, the highly sensitive person is still vulnerable to energy fields coming at her. In fact, the empath is *more* vulnerable than ever in this state.

Dealing with the toxic narcissist is exhausting for the HSP. Just being in the same room without any direct interaction can cause a sensitive person to be exhausted. The negative energy of the narcissist completely drains the positive energy of the empath. They are stealing your physical as well as emotional energy leaving you with no reserves.

After a while, the empath will feel angry, bitter, depressed or apathetic and will not be able to say why they feel that way. Even after the narcissist is no longer in the life of the highly sensitive person, the HSP will continue to have these toxic feelings for some time.

Given this physical exhaustion and loss of energy, it is easy for a highly sensitive person who is exposed to the negative energy of the Narcissistic Personality Disorder is prone to become physically ill. Nausea, headaches, inability to function or concentrate. The sensitive person might be so out of touch they just know they don't feel well. They don't know how or why. There is always the possibility that the highly sensitive person will become seriously ill from long term exposure to the narcissist.

Being in an Intimate Relationship with a Narcissist?

Even a highly sensitive person can fall in love with a person with Narcissistic Personality Disorder. Perhaps they don't know the person is a narcissist when they fell in love. Perhaps the person with NPD doesn't know still that they are that. Remember how charismatic, how charming, good looking and funny a narcissist can be. He will use the empath's sensitivity against them. He will understand how to manipulate the HSP (highly sensitive person) into falling in love before they have any idea of who he really is.

So, you fall in love before you can define your romantic interest as a narcissist. Once you realize who he is, why does the highly sensitive person stay in the relationship? It is a fact that it is not always obvious that you are dealing with a narcissist because as a narcissist they are so good at manipulation and charm. They also go out of their way to target the empath or highly sensitive person. Because the HSP cares so deeply about others, the NPD wants that person to care about him. In that way, he can use their generous energy to get attention, sympathy, praise, admiration, all those things the narcissist craves and has to have.

By the time the empath can respond, they are already drained of all their energy, they are exhausted and emotionally devastated. This state makes it harder for them to leave the relationship and the longer they stay the harder it gets. We will spend an entire chapter on how anyone, no less a highly sensitive person, can leave the relationship with a person with Narcissistic Personality Disorder.

How the Sensitive Person Deals with the Narcissist

There are times in the life of a highly sensitive person that they don't have the option of walking away or putting the narcissist out of their life. The person with full-blown Narcissistic Personality Disorder might be an aging parent, a spouse, someone you have to work with every day. In these situations, you need a game plan and some tools for survival.

- Never, ever, ever take their words to heart or let their words wound you. Never take it personally. Their words are about themselves not about you.

- Boundaries, boundaries, boundaries. We said in the last chapter that we all need to set boundaries with the narcissists in our lives. The highly sensitive person needs to set boundaries, write them down, communicate them and don't allow them to be violated. There must be consequences for the narcissist who violates them.

- Ignore the behavior of the narcissist – just walk away, don't respond, don't engage.

- Tied to the above – don't fight with the narcissist because he will always have the last word. They are bullies and they want the fight. Don't give it to them.

- Don't let the narcissist instill guilt in you because he knows how sensitive you are. He will try. Be prepared.

- Protect your self-esteem – give yourself the self-love and self-esteem that keep the narcissist at bay. Self-esteem will keep the narcissist from stinging with their words or their behavior.

- Keep track of the narcissists in your life and what they say and how they act. Write it down. How are you treated by them? Write it down. Don't allow them to manipulate you. Write it down and don't let them try to change your reality with their wrong vision.

- You are vulnerable. Admit it. Know where you are vulnerable and boost up your defenses there. Remember it is all about manipulation for them. Know that you are more vulnerable than most. Because you are an empath, because you are sensitive, you are vulnerable.

- Keep yourself educated on what is learned about narcissists and Narcissistic Personality Disorder. What are the professionals learning about this disorder? What new traits are they adding to the description of the disorder? What new therapies or treatments are they advocating? Remember how much this NPD has changed since the words were coined. Look at how much has changed since Freud and his colleagues spoke of the narcissist not being able to see others as people or objects just invisible. Stay on top of everything new about NPD and those who suffer from it.

- Remember that the narcissist does "suffer" from NPD. We need compassion. You have to protect yourself but at the same time, you have to understand there is a pain in being a narcissist.

- Take breaks from crowds or groups of people. Let your energy rest.
- Ground yourself and protect your own energy field – grounding is essential. Meditation is essential. If you are grounded and if you have protected your energy and your aura, the narcissist will not be able to drain your energy.

How to Shield Yourself from the Effects of the Narcissist

Highly sensitive people need to know how to shield themselves from all toxic people but especially from a toxic narcissist. Our last point above regarding ground yourself and protecting your energy field is a tool you must have in your repertoire to survive these attacks by a narcissistic person. How do you do this? The answer is first and foremost to create a sacred space that the narcissist is never allowed into with you.

If you live with the narcissist this may be difficult. In fact, it may seem impossible, but it is not. Having your sacred space in a public place like a library or park is not ideal but it works none the less. If, however, you are able to create this sacred space in your home or on your own property, that is best. Let's imagine that you can make a sacred space within your home. Perhaps your narcissistic spouse has a "man room". Find yourself a little corner of the home where you can have privacy, and this becomes your sacred space.

What do you need in your sacred space? Whatever makes you comfortable – perhaps some pillows and blankets. How about some candles and a music player? Perhaps you can smudge the room before you use it every time. Smudging is simply a blessing or cleansing of the space with some type of an herb. Sage is probably the most popular.

Now here's what you do in this space to protect yourself from the narcissist in your life. Make yourself an alter based on whatever your faith beliefs are. Here you are going to reflect, meditate, pray. Put articles on the alter that calm you. Put symbols of your faith or belief system on this alter. This is where you put your candles or maybe a diffuser or incense.

Take music and food with you into your sacred space. Food will be particularly important if you are either creating or raising a psychic shield. Some good food items for this are root vegetables, nuts, and juice. Have a way to play music or guided meditations and use headphones. Take a large bottle of water into your sacred space for as you work with energy you will need to stay hydrated.

The first thing you are going to do in your sacred space is to create a psychic shield to protect yourself from the negative narcissistic energy flow. This may sound strange to the everyday person but to a highly sensitive person or an empath, it is not strange at all. It is simply using the energy field to create and maintain an energy shield around yourself that the narcissist and his negative energy cannot penetrate. Of course, it takes energy to maintain the shield so you cannot have it in place twenty-four hours a day, seven days a week.

Now let's build your shield. A psychic shield will absorb or reflect energy. How you build your shield depends on the intention you have for it. Are you going to absorb or reflect? In protecting yourself from the narcissist you are going to reflect their energy back at them. This is a defensive shield and it can absorb or reflect energy, but it cannot block it or stop it. Therefore, this is work for the HSP.

Types of Shields and What They Do

1. Bubble Shield – forms a protective bubble around your body and your aura.
2. Skin Layer Shield – forms a protective shield about two inches above your skin.

As mentioned, these two types of shields either:

- Absorb energy – all the energies directed at you are absorbed by the shield and cannot get to you. The longer the duration it is in place and the more energy that hits it, the stronger it becomes. It can, however, become overloaded with energy and then put the sensitive person at risk.

- Reflect energy – all the energies directed at this shield will be reflected back but it cannot be targeted. Therefore, it can hit other things and people around you. This is still the defensive shield you want in your toolbox for dealing with the narcissist.

Now let's create the shield.

1. Go to your sacred place at a time when you know you can have privacy for at least forty minutes to an hour.

2. You are creating a reflective shield. Set that goal in your mind. You are also creating a bubble shield as it will afford you the greatest physical area of protection.

3. Get into a comfortable sitting or lying position. Begin to clear your mind. If you have practiced mindfulness before, put yourself in that state now. Become centered

within yourself. Use a guided meditation to do this if you choose.

4. Focus on drawing energy into yourself – into your physical body and not just into your spirit. For it is in your body that you feel the negative effects of the narcissist.

5. Now envision the bubble shield that looks like a mirror and reflects energy away from you. Hold that image as a mantra.

6. Remaining centered with the bubble reflective shield in your mind's eye, move the energy of the shield so that it places you and your aura inside the bubble. See yourself inside the bubble. Now make the shield harden into an impenetrable material that nothing can come through.

7. Now your protective shield is in place.

How to Lower the Shield

When you no longer need it, you should lower the shield. Simply set an intention to lower the shield and then visualize it lowering to the ground and disappearing.

Conclusion

The shield is a great tool, but it is only a tool. Use it whenever you really need it, but don't overuse it. You will get very good at putting it up and taking it down within minutes.

We know that the sensitive person cannot avoid dealing with the narcissists of this world their entire lives. We know that the person with Narcissistic Personality Disorder is a master of deception and manipulation. They tell you what you want to hear, promise you what they know you want and understand how to make you feel good.

However, it's a good bet that your "lie detector" is going off somewhere in your body when he's around. So, if you see or better yet if you feel that person across the room on his way to you is overly concerned with what he looks like, what everyone thinks about him and his status, move on. Leave the room if you have to but stay as far away from him as you can. Do not engage if there is any way to avoid it.

Chapter 8

How Can a Child Deal with a Narcissist in their Life?

We have spent two chapters on living with the narcissist and now we come to the hardest of all. Imagine being a child and living with someone they love and depend on, who is also a Narcissist. No one is more vulnerable than a child to the manipulation and abuse of the narcissist. With enough abuse, the child may grow up to be a narcissist himself.

What happens when a child lives with a narcissistic parent or another relative that they love and depend on? That child becomes wounded – narcissistic wounding – when they grow up with parents with either some narcissistic traits or full-blown Narcissistic Personality Disorder. The parents are abusive or addictive or insecure beyond what would be considered "normal" or healthy.

When living and being raised by one or two narcissistic and addictive parents, a child fails to get their emotional needs met because the focus of the house is to meet the emotional needs of the narcissist. When living with a narcissist, children do not get their early childhood needs. They might simply be ignored. They might be neglected, or on the other hand, they could be spoiled. They might be physically or sexually abused.

This child might be pretty much on their own with no one to give him guidance or structure. His has no limits. How bad childhood narcissistic injury becomes depend to a certain extent on how bad the parent's narcissism is. We realize this is a potential multigenerational problem. The parent was wounded by narcissism and now they are wounding their children in the same way.

What Happens to the Child Living with a Narcissist?

When the child cannot have his own boundaries but is meshed with the parent's adult life, they become arrested in their development and energy at the level he is when it happens. He is stuck with feelings that tell him he is unlovable, unworthy and the world is not a safe place to be. He will now carry this through his life into adulthood with this "Core Script" of narcissism.

If this child is more stubborn than most are able to see what is going on and refuse to defend the behavior of the other members of the family. This child sees the manipulative behavior, the selfish attitudes, the way one parent gives in to the other all the time. He learns this part of narcissistic behavior, develops a false self and grows up to be aggressive and intimidating himself. Then there is the guilt-ridden, sensitive child who does all he can to get his parents' love by trying to meet his parent's needs. He ignores his own true feelings and represses them because he wants his parent's love and approval. For this child, it is shame and guilt that gets locked into his arrested development. They have aggressive impulses that have not been integrated into their emotional development. They grow up to be codependent and give themselves up in relationships.

A lot of children with narcissistic injuries live in a fantasy world that is so much safer for them than the real one. They grow up to be vain, materialistic and into a vivid fantasy life. They are shallow and into soap operas, movies, rock stars, and video games. They don't develop close friendships or deep relationships because they are afraid of their feelings. Their self-esteem is so fragile they would rather live in a fantasy.

The narcissistic parent is too self-absorbed to even notice the impact they are having on their children. Even if they did would they care, or would it make him angry that his children did not live up to his image? Then what happens to the children in a nutshell:

- They begin to feel invisible – no one sees them. They might not even see themselves – have no sense of self. They end up with no ability to connect with themselves as an individual person.

- They become codependent with their own low self-esteem. They feel guilty about everything or they become narcissists themselves.

- They blame themselves for everything that is wrong in the family unit. Believing it is their fault that their parents cannot love them, and they look for ways to change themselves and make themselves worthy of their parent's love.

- They either choose to live with a narcissist when they become an adult or they choose not to be in a relationship at all. Their childhood was so debilitating and overwhelming that they cannot imagine any other kind of relationships could exist.

The Difference Between Healthy Parents and Narcissistic Parents

Let's compare the behavior of parents with Narcissistic Personality Disorder and parents that are healthy. These are the basic traits of narcissism versus a healthy parental unit.

Narcissistic Parent(s) Traits

1. They neglect their children in order to impress other people.
2. Expects his children to know what he needs and provide it instantly.
3. Only talks about himself regardless of what the conversation starts out to be about.
4. Ignores and negative effects his disdainful comments might have on you.
5. Must have the best and biggest of everything no matter what it cost the family.
6. Is always belittling and criticizing you. He always knows what is best for you and you do not.
7. Cannot see anything from any point of view other than his own.
8. Always needs

9. Always has to one-up everyone including his own young children.

10. Blame their children or spouse for everything. They are responsible for nothing.

11. Gets angry at the slightest criticism.

12. Throws tantrums and intimidates everyone in the family when he is angry.

13. Overly charming, seductive, charismatic. Vain expects admiration.

14. Fishes for compliments. Is shallow emotionally.

15. Tells you constantly what you owe him no matter what you have done for him.

16. Threatens to abandon you if you let him down.

17. Wants to make you feel inept, helpless and stupid.

18. Tells you how you should or should not feel.

19. Sees himself as above the rules/law.

20. When he hurts you, he blames it on you saying you are too sensitive and he was "only joking".

21. Might engage in physical or sexual abuse.

22. Engages in emotional blackmail.

Healthy Parent Traits

1. Allows his children to express their feelings and responds with respect.
2. Never belittles to makes fun of his children.
3. Makes sure he knows the emotional and physical needs of his children and does all he can to meet them.
4. Is able to develop intimacy and good, long-lasting relationships.
5. Has healthy boundaries of his own and respect the boundaries of his spouse and children.
6. Has priorities for his life and for his family with positive values.
7. Shares his feelings appropriately with his family.
8. Appropriately praises his children and spouse.
9. Listens to his children and spouse.
10. He/she has a healthy sense of self and values everyone in his family

How to Support Your Child When Living with a Narcissist

How can the partner or spouse make a difference for children living with a narcissist if it is not possible to remove them from the situation? Suppose you married or committed to him before you knew he was narcissistic. What can you do now? How can you protect your children?

- Learn about Narcissistic Personality Disorder in every way you can. Read what you can, call on experts, ask your physician.

- See a Therapist who is very familiar with Narcissistic Personality Disorder. See someone who is really well versed in NPD and its effects on the family. The wrong therapist could give very bad advice and cause more harm.

- Don't blame yourself – and make sure your children understand that you do not blame yourself.

- Understand the lasting emotional damage living with a narcissist will inflict on your children.

- Value your children's feelings -respect and protect. Your narcissistic spouse belittled, devalued and consistently but down the children. You need to build them back up and let them know their feelings are valid.

- Don't let the children blame themselves. There is no room for anyone to blame anyone or themselves. This is not your fault and it is not your children's fault. Explain to them why NPD happens.

- Help your children understand NPD and its causes. Tell the truth with respect.

- Get your children into a therapist for the same reasons you go yourself, except that this is even more confusing to your children than it is to you.

- Join a family support group Getting a therapist for yourself is great and you need one. But your children also need to be with you and other families that have gone through what your family is going through.

- Get your children into a kid's support group so they know they are not the only children to go through this. They need to talk with other kids who have gone through what they have.

- Don't demonize your partner. This will confuse your children even more. Be compassionate. Show your children what compassion, empathy and forgiveness looks like. As your children grow you can share more of your own experience but while they are this young it is only about them. You can find your relief with your therapist and support group. Don't share inappropriate adult information and adult issues with your young children.

- Foster a deep resilience in your children. They need to be able to face whatever happens in their own lives without effects from their experience with a narcissistic parent.

In the end, the best thing you can do for your child might be to leave the narcissistic spouse. This may or may not be possible, but if it is the best option you will have to prepare your children for this as well. However, once you have taken them out of the situation, they will recover slowly with the assistance mentioned above. They still need a therapist, family therapy and a children's support group. The odds of these things working are thousands of times better if you have your children out of the situation.

Sometimes it is simply not possible for whatever reason to get yourself and your children out of the situation. In that case, you can still follow the advice in this chapter. You will need to work around the narcissistic parent and that is not easy. You will have to assume that your children, who love the narcissistic parent, will share with that parent everything you do and say about them. So be careful but be fearless for the sake of your children.

Chapter 9

How to End a Relationship with a Narcissist

It's over. You have figured out who they are, what they are, and you can no longer remain in the relationship. However, leaving someone with a Narcissistic Personality Disorder is easier said than done. For the most part, narcissists never change because they don't believe there is anything they should change. So you trying to explain why you are leaving is not likely to sink in for the NPD you live with.

Many even go to couples' therapy, asking their spouse to change and be closer to them. They have no clue that after years of abusive narcissistic behavior, there is no trust, no ability left for the spouse to do so. Notice they didn't apologize or say they would change. They won't.

So, at this point, the only thing to do is leave. However, leaving a narcissist can be dangerous. We're not saying it is every time, but it certainly can be. You are their possession. You are their symbol to the outside world of how successful they are, what a good person they are. Anger and bitterness are likely to be their response to your left.

You, on the other hand, maybe dealing with a full-blown depression and anxiety syndrome after years of verbal and emotional abuse. Yes, you have been traumatized over all these years of life with a full-blown Narcissistic Personality Disorder. Yes, you do have Post Traumatic Stress Disorder and that is going to make it harder to leave, but you can still do it. In some cases, you have to do it. To stay with this particular narcissist would be death for you.

Why You Can't Leave

1. You believe there is hope. After all these years of trying, of giving love and being there for him, you are having a hard time giving up hope that he could change and really love you. As we know narcissists don't change. They may even pretend to change or promise they will but remember they can't. Don't fall for it. Let go.

2. The Narcissist can push your buttons – manipulate you. We know how manipulative the narcissist is. That's a major reason for leaving – to get away from that manipulation. Still, they will tell you what you want to

99

hear, promise you what you want to be changed and managed to push all your buttons to get you to stay. Even if they want to keep their promises to you, they will not be able to sustain good behavior.

3. He keeps winning you back. He will keep doing this long after you are gone so keep your guard up. He will keep using all those charming, charismatic and manipulative techniques to get you to come back. Just remember that nothing you do will change a narcissist.

How You Should Yourself Prepare to End the Relationship

Knowing you cannot change someone with Narcissistic Personality Disorder, you need to prepare yourself for leaving the relationship. Here are some things to do as you prepare or shortly after you leave. You will need support to make this happen.

- Confide in a friend or family member who you know is not going to confide in your narcissistic spouse. You feel lost and alone after years of emotional abuse from a narcissist. Confide in someone that you know that you can trust.

- Find ways to regain your self-confidence and self-esteem that's been taken from you during years of emotional and verbal abuse. Remember your own self-worth and in the future steer clear of abusive, controlling people. However, be aware that as you leave, he may get custody of all the friends and he will go out of his way to make you the bad guy. As someone with Narcissistic Personality Disorder, he cannot be seen as the bad guy in this. He needs the admiration, the sympathy and the support of your friends.

- Join a support group like Codependents Anonymous with people who will understand what you have been through. They can help you heal.

- Put a no contact rule in place and enforce it on him and yourself. It takes time to heal and if you have contact during that time you open yourself up to being manipulated into going back to him. You need to have regained your self-confidence and self-esteem before you would see him again. This takes years and you are better off never seeing him again if possible.

- See a therapist before you leave. You will need all the support you can get so put this relationship in place first.

- Once you make the final decision to go – GO! Don't hang around. Don't give him any opportunities to manipulate you.

- BE SAFE. You are dealing with a potentially dangerous person. Many people with Narcissistic Personality Disorder can be violent, mean and you just don't know what might happen. If you feel at all unsafe take measures to protect yourself. Have family and friends with you when you leave. In the worst-case scenario, you have to inform the authorities that you are leaving and ask for their oversight.

- Watch out for revenge. Narcissists are known for seeking revenge and holding a grudge. Expect something and be prepared emotionally but don't let it affect your new narcissist free life.

- Don't answer the door if he comes around after you leave. Maintain the no contact rule for at least a year if you can.

Healing after Ending a Relationship with a Narcissist

The door closes and the narcissist is gone from your life. But not from your spirit. The things they do and say have a way of staying with you for a while, impacting your self-esteem even though he isn't there to do it. It was so hard to walk away and now it will be hard to stay away and begin to heal.

The key to staying away and beginning to heal is detachment. You have to detach yourself from everything you thought you knew about him and everything you felt for him. Let go. Detachment is letting go.

Step 1: Stop blaming yourself for what went wrong and start blaming the narcissist for being incapable of really loving you. See the relationship for what it really was and see him for who he really is as someone with Narcissistic Personality Disorder.

Step 2: When a relationship ends you go through the stages of grief just as if someone died. In this stage, the anger comes. You are angry at how he treated you and angry at the abuse you endured.

Step 3: This is your stage. It is about how much stronger you are now. You're thinking positive thoughts in this stage. You feel good about the work you have done. You feel free of the love you once felt for him and now you can't stand the sight of him. You are spending more time with friends and creating a new life.

Step 4: Detachment! Success! You focus on yourself and your life now. You rarely even think about him. You are physically and emotionally free from any narcissist you might know.

What Could Have Happened but Didn't

Understand what could have happened here if we had played out an entirely different story. The ending of the story we played out was all positive. Sure, there would be pain and grief, but you would get through it. This is not how the majority of relationships with narcissists end. Here are some alternative endings that you will want to avoid.

1. The narcissists find ways to continue to betray you even after the relationship is over and you have left.

2. The narcissist makes false accusations about you. They accuse you of doing what they have done. There may even be charges filed against you.

3. Emotionally you don't recover. You live depressed, alone, resigned...People in this stage lose their careers, their family and friends. Substance abuse may come into play here. You lose interest in everything. Nothing gives you hope or enjoyment anymore.

4. You get very ill from stress and depression. Far too often we underestimate the toxicity we have been living with all these years of sharing life with a narcissist. You hold a lot of that toxicity in your own body and it can kill you. Stress raises cortisol levels and weakens the immune system. Stress can increase blood sugar levels and blood pressure levels. The result can be a heart attack, cancer, depression, stroke, and digestive disorders. Substance abuse and self-medication happen as well.

5. Physical violence from the narcissist. Though most domestic abusers are not victims of Narcissistic Personality Disorder, some people with NPD may become domestic abusers in this circumstance. This is why we have stressed safety so much in this chapter. Keep yourself safe. Be constantly aware. Live your life but don't take unnecessary chances.

6. Unfortunately, some people in this situation simply cannot handle all the stress, grief, abuse, loss of self-esteem and they feel they have no purpose or worth left. They commit suicide. Don't ever, ever, ever underestimate the toxicity that is present in a relationship with a full-blown narcissist.

Conclusion

Leaving a narcissist isn't easy. In fact, it is immensely difficult and they will do everything in the world to make you stay. In this chapter, we have looked at how the narcissist will try to manipulate you into staying. We saw what you needed to do to get yourself out of the relationship safely and what can and does happen when you don't get out of the relationship with your self-esteem intact.

Leaving the narcissist means facing your fears, your failures, admitting that he got the best of you and your dreams are shattered. It means you have to dig down deep and find the strength to come back. To be yourself no matter what. To have the courage and tenacity to get out and survive. Now you can turn your attention to helping others to get out safely as well.

Leaving the narcissist is incredibly difficult as we have seen. Now you move from living in pain and abuse to moving toward freedom and a future that is much brighter. Your broken heart will heal and so will your broken sense of self and your pride.

You have lived with cognitive dissonance for so long – believing you found your soulmate in this person with Narcissistic Personality Disorder and the opposite of knowing he is an abusive bully to you. Holding both these beliefs at the same time was necessary as long as you stayed with him. But you didn't.

You got out. You got a new life and a new start. Make the best of it and don't fall back into the same narcissistic trap.

Chapter 10

21st Century Narcissism in World Politics

In this century we see more and more narcissism in every culture around the world. It seems to be particularly true in the United States. From the "Me Generation" to the current president, it seems the byword is "It's all about me". According to Anne Manne in her book The Life of I: the culture of narcissism, there is a new type of narcissism based on wealth, a cult of self and hypercompetitive consumerism.

There is scientific proof from Manne and others that narcissism is rising, and empathy is declining. It does seem that the atmosphere we live in is ripe for a "ME" century. Technology, social media, individual pursuits and approval of putting others down enable narcissism and many times our culture more often than not, rewards narcissistic behavior.

A Narcissistic Culture

Will this create a culture, a nation, a world where some people are always right whether they are or not? A culture where you will be either charmed or belittled into agreeing that they are always right, whether or not they are? Is there an epidemic as some social scientists have claimed?

No one has the cure for Narcissistic Personality Disorder, and no one knows exactly what the cause it. As we have laid out in the early chapters of this book and say again. There are three reasons considered to cause it: a physical difference in the brain, how you were raised and by whom, and genetics. It seems to be energized and growing in today's world where the focus has moved from the group to the individual.

We see this in politics all over the world now. The question is no longer what is best for the whole. Today's question has become what is best for me. Everything about our culture says wealth, fame and celebrity. While this is happening the breakdown in face-face social interaction with others to sitting in front of a screen interacting with icons.

New studies also show that there is a new addiction out there. It is an addiction to the internet – to the screen. New studies are beginning to show that addiction to Facebook is linked to low self-esteem and narcissistic behavior. Even more serious it appears that in today's world, you need to be a narcissist to be a leader. Our culture is self-indulgent and chronically tense. Everything is trivialized by a self-serving media that turns everything, especially our politics, into a sporting event or personalities, shock value, and spectacles.

Why is there an Increase in Narcissism?

Our economics, our media, our "talking heads", all are promoting the individual, the self – not the whole. This leads to a culture that accepts narcissism as an ok way to be. Our culture lifts up the callous, the uncaring, the superficial among us as people we might aspire to be. We see this easily in the celebrity culture. Who does the media center on? Who do they put in front of us day after day? Those who seem to have the strongest "me first" identities – the divas the narcissists. People like Mariah Carey, Kim Kardashian, Kayne West, Madonna, and more.

Scariest of all – the worldwide culture appears to be set up in such a way right now that the narcissists are best suited to be the leaders of the world. Power hunger narcissists who are willing to win at any cost. Fascism spreads across the globe as these narcissists take control of the world's political systems. So many of our CEO's across the globe are narcissists. They win by selling not a legitimate, quality product, but rather a personality and false image of themselves as leaders of their companies.

Data shows that the best, most successful leadership comes from humility and elf-awareness. Yet at the same time, we are surrounded by braggadocios, self-centered narcissistic CEO's. CEOs that are raging megalomaniacs who can increase the cost of life-saving pharmaceuticals beyond the reach of the patients who need it and laugh about it when challenged.

So many of these narcissistic CEOs are running companies from one big win to the next big loss. There is more fraud in the companies the narcissists run. They are able to manipulate their employees and abuse their power.

The camaraderie between the narcissists running our companies and the narcissists running our countries is a natural alliance that only promotes more narcissism. Mass media then steps in to keep us tense all the time and cynical at the same time. Then the pop culture feeds its endless appetite for fantasies of narcissism. These fantasies lead us to elect narcissists all over the world.

What is missing, is the old fashioned belief that we are individually responsible for what we do. If we hold people responsible for what they do, narcissists would not be rewarded as they are today. Part of this is our own fault. We have given over our individual and collective responsibilities to the experts and talking heads.

This has led to a situation where about 70% of students today taking the Narcissistic Personality Disorder Inventory are scoring significantly higher toward narcissism and significantly lower on empathy than they did in the late 1980s.

Political Narcissists

In an earlier chapter, we covered a lot of famous people who were or are narcissists. An alarming number of those famous people were leaders of their countries and/or their military. From the Attila, the Hun to Donald Trump narcissists have had power out of proportion to their number and the professed beliefs of their people. This didn't begin in the 20th century it was just magnified by Adolf Hitler, Joseph Stalin, Mussolini, Douglas McArthur, Chairman Mao, Idi Amin and more.

Our leaders around the world today are more narcissistic, more self-centered, deluded and overconfident. Our leaders around the world today are more fascist, more dictatorial, more demagogic than since the 1930s. There is a natural tension between leadership and narcissism; between pro-society and selfishness. What is disquieting is how it seems that narcissism and selfishness are winning the game.

The question then becomes, can we move away from this somehow? Can we evolve toward legitimate, healthy self-esteem in our leaders? The data shows that the narcissist is not the best, most successful leader. Why do we keep electing them? The hope is that as business moves to evidence-based talent recruitment and retention, politics will follow suit. If people worldwide begin to choose leaders who actually perform better than narcissists under pressure, when the rewards are not obvious, this could change.

Can Narcissistic Leadership Succeed?

What does the science say? Is there empirical evidence on this question? Two recent studies looked at the Narcissistic Personality Inventory and asked a group of over 70 men and over 40 women to score themselves on this test. The higher the score the more narcissistic you are. The participants were then asked to work in small groups with people they didn't know. They rated each other on their leadership ability. The second study (96 men and 56 women) put people together in small groups who did know each other.

The results of these two studies showed that in the early weeks those who rated high as narcissists also rated high for leadership in the small groups. Then as the study moved into its later weeks, the ratings flipped. The people rating high as narcissists were now being rated by their small groups as the least effective leaders. It didn't take long for the narcissistic leaders to fall off the pedestal.

It was the charisma, the confidence, the charm and vision of the narcissists that initially attracted the groups to their leadership. Yet it wasn't but a few weeks before their leadership was rejected. Only if the narcissist can temper their narcissism enough to add some empathy or concern. If only the narcissist can temper their narcissism enough to not have to be right, not have to have all the answers. They have to be able to lead a team and most narcissist cannot.

In the political, worldwide arena charm, charisma, confidence will take you a long way. They won't take you all the way through. You have to be able to give as well as take. You have to be able to listen as well as talk. You have to be able to authentically care about your people.

In the long term, the people around the world and here in the U.S. need to choose leadership, that we know from the kinds of studies we mentioned above, is good for us in the long term. Not to elect someone who we like because of their charm and charisma. If we can do this, then there is hope for healthy leadership around the world.

Chapter 11

Narcissism and Sports in America

We have just seen how narcissism has invaded the realm of politics and leadership around the world. The same has been true in the world of athletic coaching on just about every level for decades. It is less acceptable today to be a "bully" as an athletic coach than it was ten years ago. Hopefully, that means that even in a "me first" culture, some things are moving away from the extreme narcissistic approach.

At the same time, narcissism has a long history in the world of organized sports. Most Americans could rattle off at least ten coaches they are aware of who either has been reprimanded for bullying or are still bullying a team in a high school or college somewhere.

Coaching in organized sports has lent itself exceptionally well to the narcissist as a career option. As you certainly know by now, the narcissist is a dominant, self-centered and manipulative personality. Narcissists emerge as leaders initially due to their charm, charisma, knowledge and in coaching the ability to win. At the same time these coaches, both male and female, at every level of organized sport, feel entitled, above the rules, and very controlling.

Narcissists in leadership positions are authoritarian, unable to accept criticism and in the realm of coaches, unable to deal with losing without hostility. They motivate through demeaning, belittling, intimidating and physical aggression. When the team wins it is because they are great coaches and leaders. When the team loses, it is because the team is a bunch of lazy failures who don't listen to the coach.

Study after study in the last 20 years has shown that the narcissistic coach can win. In fact, they almost always start out winning and win big. But just like the narcissistic leaders in politics and culture, their effectiveness fades over time and they begin to lose. It does seem that when they begin to lose is when the public turns against them and blames them for their bullying and narcissistic tactics. We'll have some specific examples of this later in this chapter.

The Sports Culture in America

The United States has always been very competitive and aggressive people when it comes to their sports. With a national identity as rugged individualists, Americans are certainly committed to their team sports with American football, basketball, and baseball leading the way. Each sport has its classic example narcissist on the professional level as a great coach. Most have these same examples on the college and high school levels, although baseball may have less or it's just that baseball is not a media darling anymore.

Professional football has seen narcissists such as Vince Lombardi for whom winning wasn't everything it was the *only* thing; Jimmy Johnson, Mike Ditka. Basketball has Larry Brown and P.J. Carlesimo, while baseball has featured Billy Martin and Ozzie Guillen.,

College sports, especially the two big ones – American football and men's basketball have certainly had and most likely still have narcissists running their programs, winning titles, and abusing kids. The big names come to mind immediately – basketball Bobby Knight, football Woody Hayes – but there are many, many lesser-known but just as abusive narcissists in the college ranks. Kelly Greenberg, former head coach of women's basketball at Boston University comes to mind.

Narcissism in Organized Sports

So why does this happen so much in organized sports? What is it about team sports versus individual sports like tennis and golf, that attracts the narcissist and allows the system to condone it? There has been plenty of research done in the field of sports psychology in the United States and the role of the team and the fans.

Organized sports is a sort of tribalism for all involved – the team and their fans. The similarities across the globe between sports and war have been pointed out many times. Often athletic competition takes the place of war beginning with the Greeks and the original Olympic Games. You have uniforms, flags, bands, fight songs, anthems, beliefs, colors, and often even bloodshed.

A perfect example of a sporting event taking the place of war in the emotions of the people in the 1980 Olympic Games USA hockey victory over the mighty Russians. Nationalism was everywhere for both teams before the game and the pride of the U.S. was almost overbearing afterward.

But this is not unusual, this is the norm. It's just that we don't "fight it out" among nations more than once every four years with the whole world watching. However, that whole world watches the Fife World Cup in soccer with just as much passion and nationalism. The U.S. and much of the world respond with the same fervor for their "team" as for their nation in the Super Bowl and NBA Championship every year. The environment in organized team sports today is perfect for the narcissistic coach to get everything they need – admiration to adoration, lots and lots of money and status, specialness, the love of the nameless crowd. Everything any narcissist could want can be had by being a highly successful, winning coach in team sports in America.

For the most part, as well, Americans did not care how you got there. Win at all costs meant it's ok to bully, intimidate, manipulate, play head games, punish, demean and shame your players. All the while the fans were "basking in reflective glory" as stated by psychologist Robert Cialdini in 1976. His work showed that fans as a whole might display some narcissistic tendencies of their own. After win fans tend to wear the colors and brand of the winner. After a loss, they do not. After a win, fans tend to talk about how "we" won. After a loss, they talk about how "they -the team" lost.

It is this highly competitive, highly rewarding culture of organized team sports that draws the narcissist coach like an irresistible magnet. Here they can be themselves and thrive. Like the fans they can bask in glory when the teams win and disavow the team when they don't.

In this environment, the narcissistic bully coach can make their actions seem normal and acceptable. They win, don't they? Everybody coaches this way, don't they? It's just the way things are done in sports and if you object it's just because you never played, you don't understand or you're just a wimp. Narcissistic behavior in coaching is ok because most coaches do it and that's the way you win. You want them to win, don't you? For the player, the choice is to just take it or walk away and be labeled a wimp themselves.

If the coach is called out on his or her behavior, the sports culture allows them to say, "I just got caught up in the passion of the moment." Well everyone in the stadium was caught up in the passion of the moment so how can you single out and blame the coach?

How Bad is it?

Just how bad is it? It seems it might be getting a little better over the past decade or so as more and more coaching abuse comes to light and the public reject it. Parents are becoming more critical of this kind of behavior towards these children and players are not keeping quiet anymore.

Yet player abuse at every level is still rampant, commonplace. Player abuse at every level is still accepted – admired even when the team representing the community wins. In the past few years, you have Mike Leach, Mark Mangino, Jim Leavitt, and Kelly Greenberg all fired for abusing players. How many more coaches do the same without any repercussions?

Coaches are the main reason a high school player chooses a certain college institution to attend and play for. The narcissistic coaches, like Bob Knight at Indiana all those years, use their charm and charisma, their ability to win and their skill at manipulation to get kids to come to their teams. Once there, the player will find out that this charming coach he thought he could trust like a father, was nothing if not a bully.

How bad is it? The line between discipline and abuse is thin. One would think that locking someone in a shed, making them run until they vomit or pass out, choking a player, headbutting a player or even "just" public humiliation have all crossed that thin line. An even bigger question is the influence that high school and AAU coaches can have on athletes in terms of their futures. The athletes may never get to face a bullying narcissistic college coach, because they may never get past their bullying narcissistic high school or AAU coach.

How bad is it? Take this one story of a high school where a fairly large group of student-athletes came forward and claimed to be "bullied" by their coaches. The coaches involved all exhibited the behaviors listed here:

- Patronizing and critical of others.
- Arrogant and self-centered.
- Expected to be treated special with special privileges.
- Expected never to be criticized and certainly never questioned by a player.
- Could not deal with being criticized by anyone, especially if they were a "winner".
- Charismatic, funny, charming, articulate.
- No respect for others privacy or boundaries.
- Cruel and abusive – targeting one player until that player quits.

- Paranoid, violent, anxious, raging when they lose or are challenged.

Does this list look familiar? Each of these coaches fit the criteria for Narcissistic Personality Disorder. This is confusing behavior to adolescents. Their coach was charming one minute and a raging maniac the next.

What makes these and other coaches narcissists and bullies? Their egos tell them they are above the rules. Their behavior is acceptable no matter what it is because the goal is to win and the institutions want to win. These coaches have no empathy for their players and think they are the "gods" of their players' world. They yell they grab, they head butt, they ignore kids, they swear, they detain, and insult – belittle their players. These are all traits of the classic narcissist. These coaches are indeed bullies and all bullies are narcissists.

Effect on Players at all Levels

What happens to the players then? Some survive. Some do not. Some give up promising careers in sports they love because of one narcissistic coach. When a player is bullied at a young age – right through college – they don't have the skills to fight back. They internalize the abuse. They believe what the coach says about them. It is all their fault. They are afraid to tell anyone what the coach is doing because that would just reinforce their lousy self-image as a coward who can't handle it.

They are ashamed. Shame is often the first reaction of a bullied kid and studies show that shame can last a lifetime no matter what is done to help the student later. This shame and lack of confidence affect their game and now they are as non-productive as the coach says they are. They are just as lacking in self-confidence outside the locker room – with grades, on dates, in their friendships. Their entire life is negatively influenced by the bully narcissistic coach. Instead of focusing on gameplay and what they can do to win, they are focused on satisfying the coach and second-guessing what they should do on each play.

Statistically, 7 out of every 10 kids quit sports because of bully coaches. We've all heard what a great influence team sports are on a child's development and future success as an adult. If these coaches are allowed to run these kids off, where are the benefits?

Here's another story of a young female athlete who loved volleyball and had done so since she was about six years old. She was a superb middle school player and had high rankings going into high school. She was looking forward to state championships, an NCAA Division 1 scholarship and a place on the national team. All these dreams were within her grasp and all were alive and well when she entered high school.

She's 34 today. She never won a state title. She never got a scholarship. She never played college ball and she never made the national team. All this didn't happen for her because one narcissistic high school coach did.

She quit before her junior year in high school and has never played volleyball again – not even recreationally. How was she bullied? The same way a middle school kid would be bullied by other kids. Her coach called her names, swore at her, ignored her, tossed gay slurs at her, grabbed her, yelled in her face and kept her after practices. She humiliated her in public every single day. Would you survive that?

Students who come forward are often bullied more by the administrators who are supposed to protect them. They must be soft if they can't take it. All these other players can take it. Besides the coach is a wonderful person. She helps kids out, gives to charity, goes to church. She charming and funny and everybody loves her. Everybody but the kid who gave up her shot at 4 years of $60,000 a year scholarship.

Can it be Changed?

The good news is that it is changing. Slowly but it is changing. Winning has become the most important thing in our narcissistic culture, but some parents are taking back their rights and responsibilities to protect their kids and their kids' future potential. Many coaches have forgotten why they got into coaching, to begin with, and because of the atmosphere too many narcissists have been drawn into the profession.

Teachers and coaches, anyone in a leadership position with children have a responsibility to protect them. Narcissistic coaches are not capable of this. The good news is that high schools and universities are no longer ignoring the players or disregarding their complaints. Bullying narcissistic coaches are being reprimanded, counseled and fired. The kids are being put at the head of the line in many places. The bad news is there are still far too many narcissistic coaches in the system and more join it every day.

Look at this shortlist of some of the most successful, most revered coaches in organized team sports history. Every one of them abused their players in some way. Every one of them was a bully in some way. Every one of them was on the narcissism

127

continuum and many had a full-blown Narcissistic Personality Disorder.

Bob Knight – Basketball – Indiana University

Mark Mangino – Football – University of Kansas

Jim Leavitt – Football – South Florida

Kelly Greenberg – Women's Basketball Boston University

Woody Hayes – Football – Ohio State University

Tom Izzo – Basketball – Michigan State University

Camryn Whitaker – Women's Basketball – Northern Kentucky University

Greg Winslow – Swimming – University of Utah

Mike Rice – Basketball – Rutgers University

Mike Leach – Football – Texas Tech University

Paul Bear Bryant – Football – when at Texas A&M

MaChelle Joseph – Women's Basketball – Georgia Tech

Many on this list are Hall of Fame Coaches and this is the tiny tip of a very large iceberg. Just as we can hope for better leadership in global politics, so can we hope to move away from narcissistic behaviors in organized team sports coaching ranks.

Woody Hayes – A Narcissists Story

Wayne Woodrow Hayes was a Hall of Fame college football coach. He served in World War II and coached as he served. Starting in 1946 at Dennison, Hayes was a head coach until 1978. He spent two years at Dennison, one year at Miami of Ohio and twenty-seven years at the Ohio State University.

Hayes won 238 games, lost 72 and tied 10 winning 79 percent of his games. He was an icon at Ohio State and worshipped throughout the entire state of Ohio. He was also a bully and a narcissist. He had a reputation for a terrible temper and physical acting out of his anger. He was known to call his players out in public, demean and belittle them in the locker room, slapping players or slugging them in the stomach.

In the era in which he coached, most people thought nothing if it. It should be noted that the era in which he coached at Ohio State was the same era in which Robert Montgomery Knight played basketball for Ohio State. Knight eventually faced the same fate at Indiana University that Hayes faced at Ohio State.

In 1972 Hayes is infamous for a tirade on the sidelines where he pushed news reporters and destroyed all the sideline down markers. Woody Hayes hated to lose and look out if you were in his way when they did. Most of the time, Hayes hit players in the shoulder pads with his bare hands. He was known to grab his players by the collar when they came off the field if he was unhappy with their play,

All of this was condoned and ignored by the administration and just accepted by his players. Yet this was classic narcissist behavior.

- He put himself above the rules.
- He was adored and admired.
- He emotionally abused his players with scorn, insults, slurs and more.
- He physically abused his players with grabs, slaps, and punches.
- He was charming and charismatic with the public.

Then came December of 1978. There were beginning to be a few rubbles about how coaches like Hayes and Bo Schembechler at Michigan and others were treating their players. There was some concern but not enough to do anything about from the administration's point of view.

The Buckeyes were facing Clemson in the Gator Bowl in late December 1978. It has come to be known as the Woody Bowl and it was the last game Hayes ever coached. He was 65 years old and had won 5 national championships at Ohio State. Yet that year the Clemson team was better than Ohio State and their defense was the difference. Clemson led 17-15 with two minutes to play and Ohio State had the ball on the Clemson 24 yard line. This was well within their kicker's field goal range to win the game.

They called what seemed like a safe play with a third and five situations. No gain would still mean a field goal and a win. It was a short pass over the middle and the quarterback could run it if the pass seemed to have any problems. There was pressure on the QB from the Clemson defense and he threw the ball right at Clemson nose guard.

Bauman caught it and ran toward the OSU sideline and the QB tackled him right in front of Woody Hayes who by now was beside himself in a rage. Hayes yelled at Bauman, "You SOB, I just lost my job". As Bauman got up, Hayes reached out and grabbed him by the back of his jersey and took a punch at Bauman's throat that did not connect.

A short ruckus between both teams' players and coaches ensued. The ABC announcers never mentioned it and coaches didn't realize what had happened until after the game. Hayes had finally crossed the line. Yet there were years of abuse toward his own players before that. His players were shocked not because Woody was physically violent. No, they were shocked because he was violent toward a player on the opposing team. That crossed the line, not the violence itself.

He called a crazy old man and age was blamed for his actions. Ohio State fired Hayes. But he wasn't a crazy old man and his actions were not a one-time thing as his record with his own players showed. Years later at Indiana Bob Knight would lose his composure in a wild rage and fling a metal chair across the court toward the Purdue bench. No one was hurt and it took another decade for Indiana to fire Knight for choking a player.

Woody Hayes – a Hall of Fame coach – a winner – a molder of men. Like Bear Bryant before him and Bob Knight after him – a full-blown case of Narcissistic Personality Disorder – put in charge of young men for over thirty years.

Conclusion

By now you should have a good sense of what and who a narcissist is. It is clear that we all have narcissistic tendencies and at some points, in our lives, we act out of them. That doesn't make us a narcissist and it certainly doesn't classify us with a Narcissistic Personality Disorder or NPD.

NPD is a mental illness classified by the American Psychiatric Association. The cause of NPD is not entirely clear as it could be genetic, biophysical or environmental or perhaps a combination of those things. Whatever causes it there is no cure and psychotherapy is the only recommended treatment. There are no drugs to treat it.

However, the person suffering from NPD is not likely to seek treatment because they think they are just fine. It is only when their world begins to crumble, or outside forces move on them that they might recognize there is a problem. As cruel and arrogant as the narcissist is, it is not really his fault. It is a mental illness.

On the other hand, there is a continuum of narcissism, as we have seen. We are all on that continuum. For some, narcissism works for them at least for a while. We see this in world politics and leadership and in organized team sports leadership. These are forms of narcissism or places where narcissism have taken root that society does not benefit from and needs ways to move on from this.

We have tried to tell you how to protect yourself from the worst forms of narcissism. What to do if you live with a narcissist. How to be an empath and deal with a narcissist in your world. How the narcissist impacts children and how we can protect them.

In all, we have tried to give you an overview of this fascinating human behavior and how you can handle it in your world.

Final Words

So, we come to the end. By now you should be able to tell who is overt and who is the covert narcissist in your life. You should be able to spot the overt narcissist fairly easily. You can see their charm and charisma offset by their arrogance and exaggerated view of their importance.

The covert narcissist is much harder to spot. They are the charismatic, charming people who always seem to have the best, know the most and have the most to offer you. Buyer beware. This is a façade and the covert narcissist is pretending to be kind, generous, and loyal when in fact they are mean, selfish, and deceptive.

The point is to protect yourself. Be armed with the knowledge you now have and choose your relationships carefully. Stay healthy and stay as far away from the person with a narcissistic personality disorder.

Extra

If you enjoyed reading this book and would like more information on Narcissism, please check out the other books by Dr Christina Covert available on Amazon!

Narcissistic Abuse: Stop Being a Victim in Toxic Relationships and Recovery from Narcissistic Mothers, Parents and Partner with Psychopathic and Sociopathic Personality. Healing from Emotional Abuse

Narcissistic Mothers: Understanding and Dealing with Narcissistic Personality in Your Family. How to Recover and Heal from Emotional and Phycological Abuse from Manipulative Mothers.

Gaslighting: Understanding the Narcissist's Favorite Manipulative Tool. Stop Being a Victim of Mind Control, Recognize Gaslight Effects in Narcissistic Relationships and Heal from Emotional Abuse

Enjoy the reading!

Printed in Great Britain
by Amazon

36073330R00087